Babajide J. Asaju
The Dynamic Equity Framework Theory

Also of Interest

Metaheuristic Optimization Algorithms.
For Local Techniques, Global Techniques, and Hybrid Techniques
Kaushik Kumar, Ritesh Kumar Singh, Sanjiv Kumar Tiwari, Chikesh Ranjan, 2026
ISBN 978-3-11-914813-9
e-ISBN 978-3-11-220729-1

Big Data, Data Mining and Data Science.
Algorithms, Infrastructures, Management and Security
George Dimitoglou, Leonidas Deligiannidis, Hamid R. Arabnia (Eds.), 2024
ISBN 978-3-11-134407-2
e-ISBN 978-3-11-134455-3

Algorithms.
Big Data, Optimization Techniques, Cyber Security
Sushil C. Dimri, Abhay Saxena, Bhuvan Unhelkar, Akshay Kumar (Eds.), 2024
ISBN 978-3-11-122800-6
e-ISBN 978-3-11-122915-7

Babajide J. Asaju

The Dynamic Equity Framework Theory

A Global Model for Algorithmic Fairness and Cybersecurity Policy

DE GRUYTER

Author
Babajide J. Asaju
Department of Computer and Information Sciences
Towson University
8000 York Rd
Towson, MD 21252
USA
basaju@towson.edu

ISBN 978-3-11-914234-2
e-ISBN (PDF) 978-3-11-222214-0
e-ISBN (EPUB) 978-3-11-222270-6

Library of Congress Cataloging-in-Publication Data
A CIP catalog record for this book has been applied for at the Library of Congress.

Bibliographic information published by the Deutsche Nationalbibliothek
The Deutsche Nationalbibliothek lists this publication in the Deutsche Nationalbibliografie; detailed bibliographic data are available on the internet at http://dnb.dnb.de.

Cover image: MF3d/E+/Getty Images
Typesetting: Integra Software Services Pvt. Ltd.

www.degruyterbrill.com
Questions about General Product Safety Regulation:
productsafety@degruyterbrill.com

Preface

Those individuals who continue to re-envision the direction of equity policies.

The present state of the world emerged through deliberate accident-free developments. A series of systems along with historical designs and previous decisions produced this current situation. These structures were developed during a period when our world had less population diversity and fewer organizational complexities. The existing stuff makes it tough while rendering possible services to the audience.

The instruments used to cope up with inequality are still there; however, it prevails owing to stagnant tools, while the changes occur everywhere.

The dynamic equity framework theory (DEFT) rose in my mind as an alternative to the existing frameworks. It works as a flexible one that fits anywhere unlike the current ones that are mere static and are no more practicable. DEFT understands that fair treatment does not work in a homogeneous manner. The system operates based on context along with changes over time and has fundamental roots in human nature. The content of this book represents my response to bureaucratic stagnation through the insertion of rigorous action and imaginative ideas.

The concepts in this work emerged from extensive interdisciplinary research together with the author's firsthand encounters in broken systems while interacting with system-impacted people. The currently served system does not entertain many crucial sectors such as education, healthcare, technology, and environment along with governance. However, with DEFT we can formulate equity which is near to the people. The design of equity systems through real-time involvement of actual people would show us what fair distribution looks like.

The book presents theoretical foundations among 10 chapters along with practical tools such as equity feedback loop theory (EFLT) and both algorithmic governance equity theory (AGET) and temporal equity shift theory (TEST). The implementation features system maps alongside data visualizations along with global case studies that support the draft of the Dynamic Responsibility Act (DRA) as a policy model for DEFT implementation.

The audience of this book consists of system builders including policy designers and students alongside everyday citizens who support purposeful justice rather than occurrence-based outcomes.

The content includes a combination of theoretical exploration with practical tools and an advocacy platform. Visual content throughout this work serves as intellectual discoveries that lead to understanding. The system faults along with their solutions are demonstrated in the diagrams.

https://doi.org/10.1515/9783112222140-202

The blueprint for the equity is that it is never ending and thus need combined efforts from all. The aim is to remake the existing systems by proper collaborations that make sure to serve all people with due respect.

A fabulous beginning of equity to be welcomed by the upcoming generations.

Let's design it, dynamically.

Babajide J. Asaju
May 2025

Acknowledgments

This book benefited from multiple academic and professional environments that supported its development. Portions of the research and conceptual framing were developed during the author's tenure as a Donald R. Beall Defense Fellow at the Naval Postgraduate School, where engagement with scholars and practitioners contributed to the interdisciplinary perspective of the work. The author also acknowledges the academic support of the Department of Computer and Information Sciences at Towson University. Any errors or omissions remain the sole responsibility of the author. The views expressed in this book are solely those of the author and do not represent the official views of any institution.

https://doi.org/10.1515/9783112222140-203

Contents

Chapter 1
Introduction – Redefining Equity in a Data-Driven World

Introduction: Presenting DEFT

In the ongoing century, the equity needs a thorough but novel reform that is essential for the modern world. For over many years, the outdated systems are in practice as various democracies use them to resolve issues related to justice and fairness. The current static management systems proved to be inefficient in addressing the modern-day requirements of the systems. The existing systems do not face the modern-era challenges of social development. The complicated systems require moving and adjustable equity systems that work on the basis of models that use principles.

The dynamic equity framework theory (DEFT) is a unique way hardly provides adjustments of moderate systems. It is an interdisciplinary framework that modernizes the equity's creation while facing social dynamics. The currently held social, cultural, environmental, economic, and technological changes are responded by the DEFT in changing global environments.

Equity is not static; DEFT views it as inherently dynamic. The equity approaches that are standard and ideal practise straight single-time ways to resolve the system-balanced errors by well-being programmes along with taxations that is distributive again and the quota system. The unique frameworks consider the individuals and communities as general blocks without counting their diversified features. In order to address the inequalities, the new frameworks take lots of time to do so. During economic recessions, both public health crises and various other systems deliver delayed or insufficient community support throughout these periods. The intended protection programmes fail to support their designated at-risk groups because the groups end up lost in the system.

The DEFT framework invalidates established methods by using an evolutionary technique for equity assessment that demands regular improvement monitoring. DEFT employs analysis of timely data from public health records and climate pattern data with employment and educational data metrics to identify instant changes in equity requirements. The purpose of delivering equity-based solutions finds complete alignment in DEFT during both theoretical development and operational deployment.

The approach functions contrary to classic hardened systems. DEFT enables systems to earn continuous feedback that initiates automatic responses when new input happens in the dataset. Equity maintains an ongoing mission that must adapt to theoretical and practical changes which occur between individual realities and cultural value modification over time.

https://doi.org/10.1515/9783112222140-001

The urban centre demonstrates housing inequality through particular distribution patterns. Official delivery of established rent assistance programmes occurs together with constructing dedicated locations for low-income housing facilities through conventional methods. The useful solutions operate with limited operational effectiveness while requiring slow distribution times. Zone-based government suggestions and neighbourhood-specific housing subsidy changes together with predictive neighbourhood stress services are potential implementations.

FACT: There exists a clear disparity in 2022 since the premier 1% of global citizens maintained 45.6% of worldwide wealth yet countless people did not have access to basic healthcare (Credit Suisse, WHO). Global warming presents the biggest threat to the 50% of population who earn the least because they produce just 7% of emissions (according to UN data). Today's crises have passed traditional equity models because of their ineffective nature.

DEFT establishes a solid stance on understanding social elements through their networked relationships with each other. The economic justice framework in DEFT analyses health disparities in relation to property values at locations where educational achievements occur. DEFT is a systems-level theory.

The approach to equity must be complete because institutions and communities and individual actors work together in complex ways. As a result of its design DEFT provides both conceptual tools and a psychological approach which views equity through systems of organizational relationships and adaptive transformations.

The main framework of DEFT transcends its applicability to governmental policies. DEFT reaches an extensive group of change agents encompassing policymakers and technologists alongside researchers and business leaders alongside activists because all these groups contribute to developing just systems. DEFT serves as a basis for instant policy execution for officials alongside a technological outline for fair artificial intelligence for engineers and researchers and as an investigative framework and advocacy instrument supported by actionable data for business executives and social activists.

The migration our society has made towards digital systems has made data-based equity frameworks necessary for immediate implementation. DEFT provides a method to achieve enduring fairness despite being incapable of delivering absolute perfection by helping systems manage complicated problems without sacrificing human dignity.

This book aims to develop DEFT that is a thorough theory that possesses dynamic environments and upcoming characteristics so that a modern era of equity can be started which is basically based on the systems that are reliable on data and design processes. Moreover, the fundamentals of the theory are proposed in this book by including practical uses to make the readers transform the real scenario of equity which is beneficial for both the existing and upcoming generations.

The Problem: Where Traditional Equity Fails

The modern-day governance as well as the social and departmental changings are normally based on equity that received global recognition over the years. It is utilized as fundamental for democracy along with social justice and economy. Thus equality hardly achieves the due purpose although it has had many years of promotion. Figure 1.1 shows the Traditional Equity Failure Cycle where a combination of factors aid each other to keep the failure cycle going while inequity continues to grow. The outdated, old-fashioned, and rigid systems keep control on equity practicability and not on the due intended purpose; that is where the problem exists. There were many models of equity that contained welfare programmes besides incentives and insurance for the hollo polloi in the time that does not work in the current dynamic world.

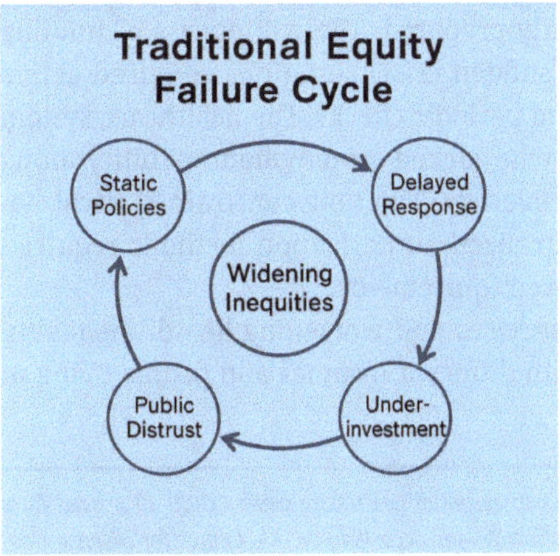

Figure 1.1: TEF cycle.

The models that are static were introduced to address the requirements of that time serve no more today. Those systems were only for the time gone and cannot be used for today's purpose. Thus, it is a dire need of the modern world to initiate the equity systems that are applicable in modern era rather than the outdated ones which used to be in those gone days.

Wealth Inequality

The previous equity systems could not check the bundles of huge amount of wealth, and that is why they had been failed. During the last 30 years the difference between wealth levels of those at the highest income echelons and those at the lowest has grown massively. Old tax systems together with loopholes in financial rules alongside fixed welfare assistance have been unable to solve fundamental structural issues of inequality. Mobility stays challenged by social systems that maintain strict aid requirement cut-offs while providing benefits which do not rise to match inflation and living costs. Modern wealth creation speeds and distribution rates surpass any capacity which earlier redistribution systems were originally intended to handle.

FACT: During the pandemic billionaires who are global secretly accumulated $5 trillion within their existing wealth while statistics from Oxfam and U.S. Census reveal significant increases in income disparities.

Healthcare Access

The static equity models revealed their absolute deficiencies to the public when the COVID-19 pandemic hit. Medical institutions from developed to developing areas suffered failures because they were insufficiently prepared. The willingness of funding mechanisms to adjust quickly failed when sudden crisis situations required active changes because they relied on past needs and periodic checks. The healthcare system failed to provide care to groups of people who lacked employment stability along with secure housing and health insurance coverage. The time-constrained fiscal nature of healthcare funding systems and centralized authorization methods required additional time to adapt to evolving healthcare requirements.

The process generated both inefficient services and worsening health inequality between racial groups and between those with different incomes and people living in different geographic areas.

FACT: The world currently divides into two regarding access to essential healthcare while COVID-19 proved fatal twice to thrice more often to Black and Native Americans than Whites according to U.S. Center for Disease Control and Prevention (CDC) and World Bank data.

Educational Disparities

Standardized educational funding methods and curricular requirements have joined standardized curricula as major barriers to systemical change. The implementation of standard educational policies creates major problems when serving students who differ from one another due to socioeconomic status and location throughout marginalized communities. Digital instructional expansion in education created new exclusion gaps when people do not have devices or internet stability or digital fluency. The use of fixed budget allocations through census-based data and generic area-based policies does not capture specific regional requirements. Traditional educational systems fail to address students who reside in rural areas or refugee camps and underprivileged urban communities because they administratively do not register these populations.

FACT: The global youth school enrolment rate in 2020 was 258 million while sub-Saharan Africa students had a measly 35% internet access (UNESCO, UNICEF).

Climate Justice

Environmental policies have gained visibility throughout the recent years but continue to remain essentially unaware of equity factors. Existing climate policy strategies completely omit concepts of climate justice that reveal environmental harm produces unequal impacts on groups of people. People living in poverty face the dual challenge of dwelling close to pollution centres and disaster zones even though they obtain scant support in both adaptation and recovery funding.

FACT: Woes triggered by climate change impact societies that emit few emissions but these groups and indigenous peoples who maintain 80% of biodiversity face systematic neglect according to the UN and IPBES.

The Deeper Problem: Static Thinking in a Dynamic World

All these failures stem from traditional equity models which operate in a reactive manner while being inflexible. The analysis uses unchanging data sources including annual reports with long-term census data and periodic assessments which fail to show the genuine fluctuations occurring in modern times. The implementation lag causes non-relevant policies because static inputs create plans that become dissynchronous with fast changes in the environment such as economic downturns and public health crises.

Decisions about many equity interventions happen in distant central locations while their community beneficiaries remain physically apart. The absent perspective from policymakers leads to incorrect resource distribution and damaged relationships between service institutions and their receivers.

The genuine essence of equity necessitates facility-based delivery. The established systems which aim to be beneficial do not contain built-in capabilities for versatility. The difficulty of achieving equitable distribution further leads to problems in timing delivery and access to services and their relevance.

The gap that DEFT aims to resolve exists in the current system of delivery.

The Context: A World in Flux

Humanity exists during a period of exceptional worldwide evolution. Modern trends including technological speed along with global climate disorder alongside shifting populations and changing social systems are creating an unprecedented interdependent and uncertain world environment. Cellular devices work together with sensors to generate data which moves through social networks and urban domains to create immediate views of human actions and requirements and ongoing developments. Modern equity frameworks operate in the same manner as analogue legacy systems by focusing on stability rather than flexibility and uniformity instead of diversity and predictability in face of uncertainty.

Our world faces dangerous inequality because different realities exist between our actual circumstances and the supposed supporting systems. Systemic inequalities persist almost unchanged even after 60 years of multiple well-meaning interventions that included welfare programmes along with affirmative action and social insurance programmes and subsidy schemes. Income inequality continues to rise. Resistance to equal opportunities grows stronger through racial, geographical, and digital differences in education and health services. The pursuit of climate justice fails to deliver its promise and hit the communities that created the least impact on global warming.

Our enduring social problems occur because the established systems operate with outdated solutions delivered through outdated methodologies. The current systems operate under obsolete assumptions while continuing to use old-value metrics together with bureaucracy-created delays. Government initiatives meant to support and empower people miss their targets because excessive rules create delays while policies become unable to understand new challenges and require excessive time to respond. The resources, allocation tools, and eligibility assessment systems which use national censuses and historical data and fixed income brackets become outdated before they can be used effectively. A delayed time frame in equity delivery systems results in significant gaps when delivering services.

FACT: Statistics from Statista indicate that 120 zettabytes of data global data was produced in 2023 but most equity frameworks continue to function with outdated procedures. Columbia University and ILO research showed numerous individuals dropped out of welfare during COVID-19 which proved that strict systems collapse during emergency situations.

The world witnessed the extent of failed system delivery due to COVID-19 pandemic. Millions of people in both wealthy and poorer international realms discovered gaps in the so-called robust social security systems. Support systems and help reached informal workers too late because these workers alongside freelancers from the gig economy as well as immigrants and individuals without digital access faced invisibility within such systems. The virus's transmission occurred in real time; yet the reaction took too long and failed due to uncoordinated programmes and incorrect targeting, thus exposing the deadly problems of equity models built for static conditions. The static structure of welfare eligibility policies demonstrated inadequate speed in responding to evolving on-ground needs of the crisis.

The volatile business landscape makes it imperative to develop a new equity paradigm which has become necessary rather than a suggestion. This system never simply redistributes assets periodically; instead it automatically and intelligently reacts to actual world circumstances. The novel equity system is possible through DEFT. The framework should address and utilize the existing changes in technology along with structures of data so that the fairness standards can be established for the upcoming era.

Introducing Core Concepts

DEFT's core theme involves understanding both its concepts and their operational dynamics. The equity is viewed as an evolving procedure by the DEFT that adapts the changes in the external environment. It considers the equity as an ecosystem rather a mere transaction, as a flow rather than a formula. Figure 1.2 outlines the core components of the DEFT framework. It shows how the components that will aid in the achievement of the equity principles over time. The framework should entertain every individual and balance the social system that is equally accessible.

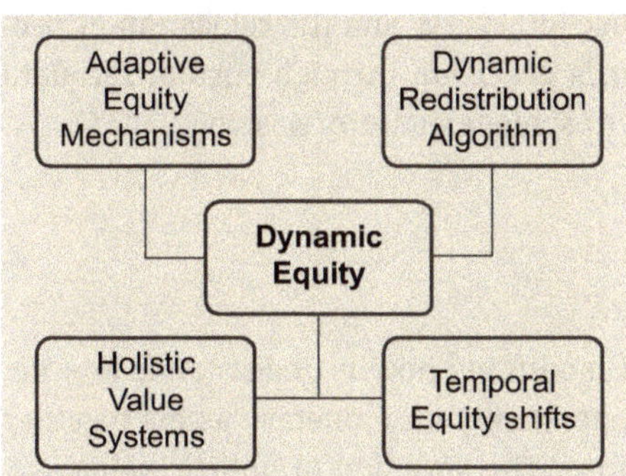

Figure 1.2: Key DEFT concepts.

Dynamic Equity

The dynamic equity is the fundamental of the DEFT. The equity works as dynamic process in this new view, as it goes ahead of the old single-time solutions with similar policies. The dynamic equity is applicable as it adapts to the must-needed changes that normally do occur in the social, economic, cultural, and technological perspectives.

A dynamic equity system determines fairness across different population groups through changes in circumstances and it considers time-span effects. Such a system possesses capabilities to hear inputs alongside learning from them to develop calibration adjustments which lead to system balance. The framework identifies the new fairness metric with respect to “Static Equity”.

Adaptive Equity Mechanisms (AEMs)

The principles based by the DEFT are put forward by the adaptive equity mechanisms (AEMs). The AEM points out the cultures that lack in food owing to crops damage by the climate changes. The constituted authority exhibits low level of productions as suggested by different systems. With special reference to enforcement strategies, it has been found that the climate change mechanisms give direction to such behaviours. By these systems, friction is reduced and bias is eliminated, encouraging collective society.

Dynamic Redistribution Algorithm (DRA)

The innovative characteristics are used by the dynamic redistribution algorithm (DRA) in order to further proceed the intelligent workouts where it holds the resource redistributions processes. The DRA includes both the personal as well as the collective equity profiles which makes it different from the traditional systems and it also uses the real-time analysis which makes it unique.

The system is also beneficial in pointing out the multiple changing problems such as health changes, environmental modifications, job losses, and the relocation of people. The redistribution scheme evolves towards precision through customized data points that erases group-based methodologies to achieve better precision.

Holistic Value Systems (HVS)

DEFT performs a substantial growth through modifying how it understands and defines value. The majority of current equity systems rely on monetary assets together with economic results for their core foundations. The adoption of holistic value systems (HVS) by DEFT improves limited viewpoints by creating a broad and inclusive approach to detect valuable social components. The HVS enables system development that assesses previously unknown forms of capital which include cultural understanding along with emotional workforce investment and family nurturing activities and environmental conservation methods and social network strength and digital accessibility. AEMs perform monitoring of equity requirements through existing data streams from varied sources combined with survey data and mobile data and IoT sensors and economic indicators to achieve policy change. AEM performs automated food security area scans at climate change regions with crop failure incidents to deploy emergency funds and modify aid limits and establish mobile distribution sites before official approvals are processed. The mechanisms help reduce delays and friction because they remove human bias from equity decisions which leads to better distribution of fairness between groups.

Target Audience

Policymakers

Through DEFT policymakers gain access to a completely fresh framework, and they need to develop inclusive governance systems that respond to everyone. The DEFT methodology gives policy creators tools to produce adaptable rules that adjust their operational boundaries by processing real-time community data as well as time-sensitive information. The responsibilities of policymakers extend across schools and hospitals and they can maximize their use of DEFT to build multiple objects that reveal potential dangers and potential protection methods. This system enables administrators to transform their reactions from delayed and general to quick and specific managerial choices.

Technologists

Technology experts remain responsible for applying DEFT principles into operational work through their professional activities. A mixed group of AI developers and platform architects and data scientists and software engineers will execute this initiative. The responsibilities of technologists primarily include adding ethical algorithms at development stage while they establish methods to check fairness and transparency procedures. With the help of DEFT system builders can make platforms that locate bias and lower its impact rather than letting bias become more intense.

Researchers

The DEFT also helps the researchers who conduct various research activities of sociology as well as economic developments to perform the data analysis. The core beneficiaries in research of the DEFT are the sociologist, economic scientist, and data scientist who conduct their research while looking for solutions to the problems in public health as well as other sectors.

Business Leaders

The businessmen along with the entrepreneurs are helped by the DEFT framework that offers them the most ethical and the long-lasting paths which prove and encourage the inclusion throughout their functional activities. The DEFT framework also encourages the different businesses to implement the equitable procedures into their possible decision-making processes such as recruitment policies and the product development stages along with corporate social responsibility activities. DEFT enhances the businesses by offering them the pathway to go beyond the basic outcomes of the CSR activities and making the profits along with social welfare.

Activists

The different organizers and activists utilize that the DEFT is their core supportive system because their activities are to promote justice and human rights. In this case, the DEFT makes them able to enhance the moral ethics and become advocates of the ethical practices by making networks with the data reset systems and helping in developing the solutions. The system demands the public and the relevant people to work for the betterment of the society and normalize and regulate the equity practices and daily life usage.

Why DEFT Matters

The framework helps in finding the solutions to the present-day complicated global problems in a real structured manner. The equity remains there in the modern world because of the continuously occurring changes and underestimated situations that arise among the multiple crisis. The most unique aspect of DEFT is its ability to adapt to the social changes and the technological changes and enhancing framework for the fairness.

The DEFT makes it possible to fix the exact data analysis systems in men's ethical system that sets the individuals as their major focus. DEFT works as a force to the existing system which is out-dated and lacks many crucial points such as technology, ethical responsibility, and many others. Designers built these systems with minimal self-adjustment functions which become inadequate under high-pressure conditions.

Through DEFT the approach turns away from static equity views to view fairness as a result that needs modification based on current information and present social developments and cultural changes. According to the framework complexity functions as the essential source which drives systems' adaptable features. The more variables, the more insight. The more change, the more potential for refinement.

Conclusion

The framework of DEFT emerges as an adaptive and responsive tool during present times which combine racial and economic equality issues alongside real-time policy creation and artificial intelligence-based societal bias constraints. DEFT creates an atmosphere which encourages all stakeholders including government professionals alongside technology developers and researchers and business operators together with civil society members to discard traditional solutions and uncomplicated approaches. With DEFT we should welcome the implementation of live learning processes together with ethical data solutions and time-specific solutions that address local needs.

The primary importance of DEFT comes from reshaping how we understand equity should function. The definition of equity moves beyond fixed criteria and becomes an active element that takes place during progress. It establishes itself as the fundamental operational basis which developers embed inside designs of institutions and technologies during their initial conceptual phase.

The book advocates for an alternative understanding of equity which is presented as an active system that adapts with human development while remaining favourable to present identities and future aspirations.

Chapter 2
The Problem with Static Models

Introduction

The practice of equity implementation throughout recent history has predominantly built its approaches on fixed systems. Government institutions implement programmes of welfare with affirmative action and redistributive taxation to decrease social gaps between high- and low-income groups through methods that are becoming obsolete. Analytic models function by using predetermined criteria and fixed dataset to implement non-specific solutions that cannot respond to current social evolution and technological and environmental adjustments.

The intervention methods of these systems persist as uniform applications across long periods despite changing social demand. Modern economic shifts as well as technological industry transformations take place too swiftly to match the assumptions of static equity systems while pandemics and climate disasters emerge drastically.

The research traces the development of static equity systems from their creation until their current implementation challenges. Actual examples from markets show static systems fail to work so this work develops an adaptive model comparable to the adaptive system (DEFT) implemented here.

The use of static models as policy tools for equity lost its effectiveness because it became necessary to define them and analyse their historical significance within this field. Welfare systems of past economic depressions designed safety nets for unemployed elderly people together with disabled individuals. Affirmative action policies stemmed from civil rights movements to close the discrimination gaps that separated racial and gender groups in educational enrolments and work-based recruitment. Tax-based redistributive models developed when society believed that wealthy persons together with corporate entities should give increased financial support for public welfare to enable governments to supply crucial services for vulnerable populations.

The social models proved successful in their historical period by delivering necessary assistance and creating development opportunities for social development. Their achievements witnessed success during periods of social stability because economic stability along with societal conditions disappeared. The present-day world maintains two defining characteristics, which are volatility and complexity. The ongoing welfare traditions in countries do not prevent rising economic inequality between citizens. Modernity has introduced new racial and geographic forms of social inequality alongside demographic elements that block minorities from obtaining equal access to healthcare and education and job opportunities. Static policies also fail to address digital inequities even though they were developed to resolve previous social challenges.

https://doi.org/10.1515/9783112222140-002

What makes static systems inherently weak is their lack of adaptability feature. The criteria established during the last decades prove inadequate for someone who becomes unemployed because of automation or who needs support after being forced from their home because of climate change. The systems fall short when it comes to performing real-time responses. The evaluation process for policies together with their revision and implementation takes place after the conditions they were intended to address have shifted substantially.

Equity receives one-time treatment within static models because such systems prioritize static solutions rather than continuous equity management. These initiatives usually focus on achieving equality in one particular point in time yet ignore the subsequent modifications that occur to the environment. Sustainable and recurrent adjustment of equity remains outside the scope of this approach. A scholarship programme meant to help low-income students gain higher education access at first improves their educational opportunities yet such students face future difficulties with graduation and finding employment after college because the programme lacks continued support and adaptation.

Static models that use outdated data also maintain strict and rigid operating systems. Policies are usually built based on historical patterns along with past census information while showing slow responses to current conditions. These delays cause interventions to reach after critical periods and without matching present requirements. Annual reports do not detect immediate outbreaks or population changes that affect healthcare resource distribution. Environmental policies based on climate models which are a decade old will not be effective against modern emerging threats and localized environmental impacts.

The mismatch between actual circumstances and policy goals allows problems to emerge which results in effectiveness reduction. Support arrives too late for communities facing the highest need while these communities may never receive the assistance at all. Bureaucratic inefficiencies create additional hurdles because organizations have too many approval stages and their implementation differs from region to region and their agencies work without coordination.

Equity evaluation models that operate statically fail to take into account the various aspects of equity in decision-making. Such approaches concentrate on financial poverty yet neglect to analyse how cultural assets and emotional work as well as environmental rights affect the situation. A restricted view creates both insufficient results in addition to supporting existing inequalities in the system. Digital education and language support deficiencies within employment training initiatives result in exclusion of participants who need such help.

Modern conditions surpass the ability of static equity models to manage their complexity because of rapid changes in the world. Due to their limited adaptability and long response times and restricted angle of perception, they demonstrate inadequate capability to solve the multiple challenges of the current century. The world needs an adaptive model of equity that operates dynamically with the flow of its target environment through real-time learning capacities.

Explaining Static Models

As per equity models, the intervention aspects respond to resolve the issues of social inequality. Social changes occurred at great place the models kept on developing over the time. The major in behind the establishment was to ameliorate the population and enhance equality across groups. They proved to be flopped as they could not fit in the modern day problems. Therefore, static models must be studied further to understand their limitations.

1. Affirmative Action

Affirmative action is against the biasness on the basis of the discrimination and arose during the twentieth century. Moreover, its aim was to prevent people from being discriminated on the basis of race and gender particularly in education and employment. The policies explain lucid aims and opportunities for the minority groups to gain equal recognition and representation.

2. Redistributive Taxation

It is one of the core systems that the governing body utilizes to return economic equal goals. The high-income holders are charged progressive tax rates to enhance revenue system to serve the undermined groups and fulfil their due needs. They are provided equal rights and opportunities with the help of such systems.

From a theoretical standpoint, the system functions as protection against economic deficiency and closure of social gaps. The system operates with multiple severe operational challenges in real-world applications. First, it is fundamentally slow. Benefit payments through tax assessments occur annually or quarterly at times but fail to meet immediate needs of recipients. When economic volatility threatens like recessions and pandemics and mass layoffs occur redistribution schemes in place tend to respond too late.

FACT: United States household wealth statistics reveal that the top 1% of citizens managed 32.3% ownership in 2021 when compared to 23% control in 1989 even though tax structures were set up progressively (Federal Reserve Survey of Consumer Finances).

The framework of redistributive taxation applies to an economic structure that shows minimal changes in income distribution from one year to the next. The gig economy has shifted such assumptions because people commonly alternate between different types of employment and joblessness. The restrictive process of deciding who gets benefits and when fails to recognize the income irregularities of people whose financial patterns are not traditional.

3. Government Aid Programmes

Government support programmes that include food stamps together with disability benefits and both housing assistance and education subsidies provide essential components of static equity models. The programmes establish clear requirements for recipients and allocate resources following their predefined rules. The system aims to give essential support to those in need and establish equality between everyone affected.

The Indian administrative welfare systems face problems and issues and the system of delivery. It takes lots of time to proceed the applications of beneficiaries. The trust among people is lost because of the limitations the system has in accessibility and know-how about the distribution and the standards of the programme.

The systems do not have the ability to contain the frameworks and mechanisms that adopt to the changing environment. The aid programmes are designed on the basis of political campaigns during the elections rather than on the basis of needs of the people. This administrative structure and funding process undermine the program's ability to meet quality goals.

Limitations of Static Equity Systems

These systems mainly lack the sustainability in the current modern era. Their fundamental operational weakness makes them unprepared for adapting to the present day dynamic conditions in society. Such issues transcend theoretical investigation. The formal operational systems generate direct life-altering results as they create higher inequities between beneficiaries and non-beneficiaries while leadership groups become more agitated about seeking alternative solutions. The text analyses four main deficiencies of static equity systems, which are described throughout this work.

Lag in Responsiveness

The biggest disadvantage of static systems emerges when they fail to serve up immediate operational results. The majority of governmental redistributive tax policy decisions and fixed healthcare subsidy programmes react slowly by analysing past events after they occur. All eligibility-based welfare programmes work with this method. The information collection process happens at infrequent intervals when the systems use this data to make decisions that result in decisions based on outdated information. Most unemployment insurance systems illustrate this phenomenon. Unemployment assessment typically depends on 1-month income and employment data but ignore current employment loss and essential needs or financial difficulties. A large number of unemployed Americans experienced long delays when they sought pandemic relief through outdated administrative systems that prolonged their eligibility assessments. Policies designed to address existing conditions prove inadequate to reach a problem between their implementation date or when modifications become necessary. The extended duration of equity programme implementation along with economic and environmental and technological and social disruptions results in minimum targeted outcomes that could generate negative effects.

Overgeneralization

Standardized equity systems choose policies by grouping large groups of people while using programmed response tools. The case of educational equity functions as an outstanding illustration to demonstrate this issue. The current funding system for schools depends on district-wide average statistics instead of considering individual student demographics particularly in support of disabled learners and English learners and students from low-income families. The method of distributing extra funding through standard increases seems equal on the surface; however, it generates larger division between students attending underprivileged educational facilities. When individuals who pay taxes consider system to be equitable as well as assume that the authorities applying the laws are non-bias and consistent, they obey willingly. Other components that are as well important in discouraging tax evasion include enforcement which can entail the use of penalties and chances of being caught.

Lack of Feedback Loops

The oldest and most severe flaw of static systems exists in their lack of internal feedback systems that should provide valuable information. A policy becomes operational after implementation where it remains basically unchanged for multiple years despite any changes to effectiveness or relevance. The fast evolution of the operating environment makes such problems even more acute.

Any initiative to promote equity fails to detect its actual impact when monitoring systems remain static and real-time data integration and learning systems are absent. They cannot self-correct. Most equity initiatives unintentionally create the same inequalities which they were designed to address.

Consider disaster relief funds. The post-disaster aid distribution system depends on using out-of-date census information and local damage calculations instead of instant need inspections. Better funding resources reach those communities that have access to money or possess higher social standing than underserved populations. Organizations do not typically track or use feedback regarding success rates or drawbacks together with beneficiary identification to enhance their future activities.

The system remains unable to develop essential capabilities that would allow it to evolve adjust to changing circumstances. Institutional policymakers continuously develop reactive approaches which maintain equity in a perpetual pursuit of the problem instead of proactively forming outcomes.

The Cumulative Effect

These weaknesses collectively reduce the operational effectiveness of static equity models. When multiple weaknesses merge into one another, the result becomes a system that operates slowly with broad but inefficient processes while requiring outdated methods. Such systems function poorly in operational settings requiring rapid adjustments and detailed adaptation capabilities. They also need to learn from feedback. Such systems cause both public trust to decrease and substantial resource waste while failing to fulfil their basic fairness principles.

Using static equity systems within the given context simultaneously deteriorates both efficiency and fairness of the adjudication process. An alternative approach to equity demands a fundamental change in fairness thinking by adopting a developmental framework instead of seeing it as a static outcome.

The Dynamic Equity Framework Theory (DEFT) offers a new foundation for reimagining equity.

Case Studies

Healthcare Access During COVID-19

FACT: CDC COVID Data Tracker reveals that Black American hospitalizations for COVID-19 were 2.9 times more frequent than those of white Americans in 2020.

The Coronavirus pandemic conducted a worldwide test of public health systems which demonstrated how both healthcare systems and structural parts of static equity models showed their fundamental weaknesses. Healthcare facilities throughout the world collapsed while facing record-breaking healthcare demand levels. Numerous countries amongst the most developed had to rush for the allocation of vital life-saving equipment including ventilators, ICU beds, and personal protective equipment (PPE) alongside vaccinations. The processes responsible for resource distribution depended heavily on static mechanisms, which included fixed funding methods together with previous usage patterns and administrative approval polices.

The early pandemic distribution of ventilators relied on healthcare records from before the pandemic against what became the actual epicentres of new viral spread. The pandemic's case growth hit urban zones and essential employees who frequently belong to underrepresented communities yet distribution policies adhered to previous health statistics and infrastructure calibration procedures. The COVID-19 crisis exposed severe medical equipment shortages in cities like New York City and Northern Italian areas but many different places maintained extra stockpiles.

The processes for testing as well as vaccination access stayed within inflexible systems. During the initial COVID-19 pandemic, testing facilities predominantly located in affluent areas where healthcare institutions already existed in the United States. Previously many rural residents of lower income and minority backgrounds suffered healthcare discrimination because they received insufficient testing access through their inadequate healthcare system. The matriarchal family homes of these groups became their primary residence as they worked essential jobs with multiple health issues but received substandard pandemic care because nonsituational regulations restricted their access.

During this particular era, the insurance industry failed to show adaptability. Staff who lost employment during lockdowns became ineligible for health insurance coverage precisely when medical support was most necessary across locales where insurance benefits depend on employment. The existing public insurance together with welfare schemes lacked the capability needed for governments to implement speedy transformations. A protracted amount of time passed before emergency aid reached applicants because they experienced complex and inconsistent documentation standards without sufficient translation support.

These systems achieved dismal outcomes which led to sustained high death rates occurring between different population groups. The COVID-19 pandemic took many more Black individuals and Indigenous people and Latino people living in the United States compared to their proportion in the population. Through solid government legislation, both slum residents and refugees alongside undocumented labourers received zero benefits.

Climate Change and Environmental Injustice

In the pandemic time 2019, the vulnerability of the static systems demonstrated issues of the global climate change. The climate change increases across years at slower pace; however, it grew faster since the beginning of the century. The existing systems do not necessarily need this approach but the system still prevails with the originality. Moreover, the strategic planning is needed for the global warming as well as environmental injustice.

The long-term planning of this policy system is need of the hour to resolve the global concern. Furthermore, while vast research exists on climate change, there is indeed a lack of empirical and theoretical literature through which either individual aspects of global warming or a combination of various factors is analysed holistically with respect to the different dimensions. The authors recognize that this is an area that has not been investigated in this comprehensive manner; this gap should be filled by exploring the multiple links of the specified variables and consequently the overall effects on environmental injustice. It should include primary data in an effort to produce accurate policy interventions for the enhancement of the sustainability. The results of this framework should be beneficial to the concerned authorities and policymakers as they provide an opportunity to understand gaps and invent better approaches to eliminate the problem of climate change.

The World Bank together with the Green Climate Fund allocates assistance through long delays and demanding project milestones and regimen standards which ignore locality options. Figure 2.1 highlights the factors that cause and perpetuate the rigidity of static systems in times of crises, leading to SEM failure. This situation affects communities throughout the Global South as they lack both the necessary political power and organizational abilities needed to fulfil the requirements. The outcomes of this aid either reach far too late the moment of need or the assistance disregards the developing requirements on the ground.

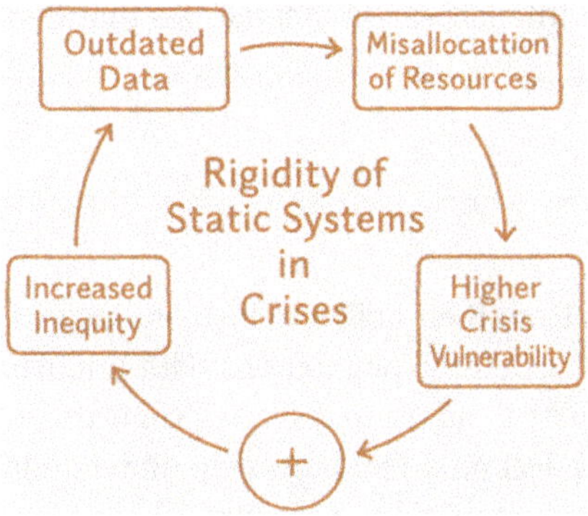

Figure 2.1: SEM failure.

Climate models along with environmental impact assessments rely on old-fashioned datasets that fail to incorporate modern weather pattern transformations and changes in land use and community defence weaknesses. Inappropriate funding allocations become apparent when seawalls receive resources to protect areas but the people in heatwave-affected inland areas go without appropriate drought management.

The practice of ignoring local knowledge during policymaking processes helps to maintain environmental injustice. Indigenous people have accumulated numerous years of experience responsible for environmental protection. Static systems choose to rely on academic and governmental information instead of what individuals actually experience. The exclusive reliance on certain types of knowledge causes minorities to have less influence over developing adaptive solutions.

The environmental needs of the twenty-first century need policies able to shift resources dynamically and process hyper-local measurements as well as learn from resulting performance numbers. Static systems as a matter of their inherent design parameters cannot achieve this level of changeable functionality. Their structure matches an outdated world model.

Real-time adaptable systems that learn and adjust according to situations are the only systems that can deliver successful outcomes to their primary users. These case studies confirm without doubt that an equity model similar to DEFT needs immediate implementation because it understands complexity as a prerequisite for developing thoughtful and compassionate design systems.

Implications of Static Systems

The continuous application of static equity systems, which depend on permanent policies coupled with pre-established data collections along with strict benchmarks, leads to extensive consequences, as illustrated in Figure 2.2. These systems that initially demonstrated progression through well-meaning construction have become less useful due to their rigidness which cannot accommodate modern complex environments. The persistence of such systems throughout time intensifies the inequalities that they had previously hoped to minimize.

Exacerbating Inequality

The main destructive effect of static systems stems from their ability to increase inequalities with the passage of time. The models were created for populations with uniform characteristics and stable environments yet lack ability to adjust to emerging contexts.

The process makes it easy for institutions to select only residents who understand bureaucratic systems and this discrimination isolates marginal communities made up of less educated and underprivileged members.

Public education funding distributions using fixed formulas allocate resources through outdated student enrolment statistics together with census data from previous times. Educational institutions in swelling communities alongside changing economies face prolonged financial shortfalls because official funding changes take an indefinite amount of time. Resource adjustments sometimes fail to materialize in any way. Stable regions that have powerful districts experience rising resources while unstable communities remain underfunded. This unnoticed funding gap grows through time because passive infrastructure systems maintain inequality by passive means.

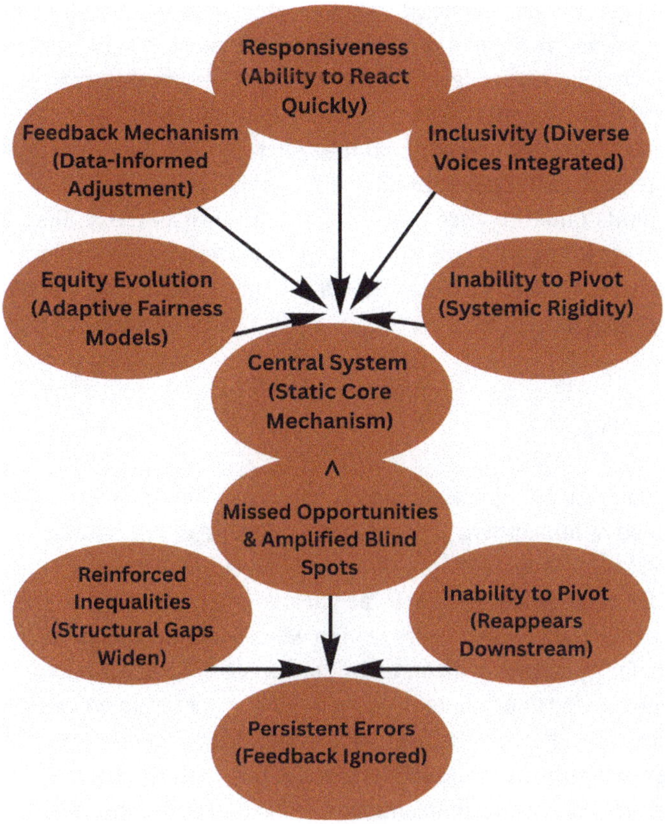

Figure 2.2: Flowchart of practicality of static systems.

Tax redistribution protocols contain progressive features on documentation, though these systems do not gain backing from informal workers including sweepers and people without official identification. The exclusionary policy creates a system where none of the affected population gets access to benefits, which intensifies poverty and exclusion problems.

Erosion of Public Trust

The use of outdated systems provides unfair outcomes that enhance doubts in the people's minds and trust fades away. The time delays in the social setting structures offer people become sceptical about the systems and the institutions. All this results in declining public interest and trust of the people which ultimately have major consequences such as declining public faith, people engagement, and sharp resistance towards constitutional changes in the system.

Take the example of relief systems of the government during disasters. The philanthropist efforts are carried out to rescue the public. However, some people are left behind, and some experience delays. This develops some serious results about the priority and the integrity of the government. The consistent failures finally develop a sense of biased performance of the government and the general public perceives it as a failure and the incompetence and the vulnerability of the government officials.

The different departments failed to encourage and ensure transparency, that is why the people lost their trust in the government. The systems work on the outdated version causing more loss in trust among the people. All this, ergo, results in continuous decline in the way of people trust.

Reduced Impact and Scalability

Static equity systems demonstrate a major weakness because they fail to access sufficient abilities to make effective impact when needed most. Emergency situations bypass normal evaluation cycles for static systems since they develop too quickly while demanding swift adaptable emergency responses at various scales. Real-life occurrences that appear outside policy scheduled times lead to weaker impact potential.

The combination of eligibility criteria with standard health measurements in public health programmes becomes ineffective in identifying population requirements today. The lack of proper communication between current emergency settings and public policy measures creates potential death casualties in instances of fast-moving health emergencies and natural disasters. Post-event or mismatched development assistance becomes useless for most situations but turns damaging when its timing is wrong.

The systems do not reach their emergency scaling objectives because they were not built to handle such situations. The limitation of public assistance programmes through budget quotas results in incapacities during unforeseen economic downturns or natural emergencies that produce assistance interruptions and delayed distribution of funds.

Perpetuation of Institutional Inertia

The sectors that utilize the static versions enhance the departmental routines that normally prioritize compliance over the performance satisfaction. The aim of the above said is to give a clear comprehension on the factors that lead to climate changes and environmental injustice. In its empirical core, it aims to contribute practical solutions and policies for fighting global warming employing direct data analysis in order for it to support governmental policies and enhance the trust of the public on environmental injustice. Through the clarification of all those interrelationships, the framework will make the contributions toward the proper understanding of the causes for climate changes and design the sound future measures to prevent the earth and to promote the environment friendly initiatives.

Counterproductive Consequences

The studies were conducted and most of those have analysed different elements that support climate change and environmental injustice; however, more comprehensive study that takes into account legal, social, cultural, and economic factors together is needed. This system aims to fill the gap by analysing the nature of injustice that is complex and providing efficient policy interventions to enhance sustainability. This study also with the help of literature review and primary data analysis aims to provide valuable thoughts to the concerned authorities and legal representatives to effectively reduce global warming and carbon emissions. Besides, the educational aid provided through the same and unified testing results in rote learning undermining the potential of the students.

Setting the Stage for DEFT

The fairness frameworks established before relaxed periods and specific circumstances have proven inadequate for current societies because they fail to deliver suitable answers for advanced dilemmas. Social inequality reveals itself through numerous points throughout the world because of frameworks that were intended for justice progression yet never evolved.

Our critical challenge today stems from the absolute importance of equity which we cannot question anymore. The present question is about the usefulness of our current models to deliver equity results. As this chapter demonstrates more and more, the answer reveals itself as no. These systems remain outdated because they serve as active barriers that prevent the delivery of progress. The systems now operate as obstacles because they lack the capability to handle real-time demands and demonstrate diverse population realities and process current data which guides better intervention strategies.

DEFT represents an evolutionary necessity beyond a new model within this context. The DEFT starts functioning after static structures cease their operation. The framework preserves existing structural frameworks from previous equity work and then eliminates their static characteristics and heavy-handed management style. The framework establishes a system in which the static needs from past frameworks are removed and the adaptable are placed in their due respective place. DEFT creates a system where fixed requirements from previous models are replaced with adaptable criteria. DEFT delivers its outcomes right away since traditional policies need extensive time for adjustment. Dynamic systems at DEFT operate through population-specific solutions generated from current information and environmental conditions.

The main strength of DEFT results from its combination of data science and systems theory together with behavioural economics and ethics and human-centred design. The system bases its operations on the reality of human diversity instead of assuming standardization for all people.

The world faces new persistent problems, which include job sector disruption from automation together with AI discrimination and geographical climate risks and worldwide mobility transformations during pandemics. The various disturbances result in transformations of both need's physical form and its geographical distribution. A responsive equity system needs both detection capability to spot changes in social needs and compassionate methods for meaningful action. The designers specifically developed DEFT for this function.

This statement should make it clear that the author does not discard all previous models. Social fairness for society materialized through the combined implementation of affirmative action with redistributive taxation and welfare programmes. But their contributions are incomplete. These successful models need additional advanced follow-up systems to achieve full success. DEFT advances past previous frameworks by creating an enhanced formulation of its purpose for contemporary digital worldwide data-centric realities.

Future chapters provide details about DEFT's structure including an explanation of its operational procedures and domain-wide deployment techniques. DEFT requires immediate deployment to address various real-world systems including healthcare institutions together with school systems and urban growth projects and organizational decision systems.

The concept fits beyond organizational structure functions by providing a conceptual foundation. The time requires coordinated approaches between leadership and policymakers and technology developers as well as community organizations to establish new systems free from traditional control methods. The youth of this generation needs competent data and the due capability of the equity understanding. Citizens are obligated to adopt innovative practices as it stands for the fulfilment of their civic responsibilities. The dynamic aspects in context lay foundations for the fair and fine systems.

The statements lack evaluation of present-day situations. Modern systems need to handle complex environments rather than try to simplify them when functioning in our current complex environment. Policies proving success need to operate their listening and speaking functions with equal adaptability as their enforcement abilities. Static equity models are now outdated because they successfully progressed our advances to a specific level. Static equity models maintain inertia through their usage currently causing the waste of valuable resources and enable many fatalities while absorbing vital time periods.

DEFT begins its mission to create better contemporary outcomes that will prepare the system for upcoming demanding requirements. The DEFT system merges evidence with innovative thinking through tested principles that produce successful outcomes in a forward-looking manner.

Our institutional systems need flexible solutions because the rapid changes in the current environment exceed their ability to adapt. Modern adaptive systems forming from their environment will dominate the future.

Chapter 3
Core Theories of the Dynamic Equity Framework Theory (DEFT)

Introduction

The following chapter provides the key points and the details of the nine core theories that are fundamental in the development of the dynamic equity framework theory (DEFT). These basic theories offer mental and functional perspectives to the DEFT to make it a changing approach in the way of equity in the current era. To do with particular equity perspectives that contain justice and governance, the theories are discussed one by one. The DEFT is being polished with these theories not only to make it applicable theoretically but also to offer practical solutions to the ever-growing problems in the educational, healthcare, climate policy, technology, and economic sectors. The DEFT's strong way-out is built by these theories to cope up and make way in the modern world.

Real-Time Redistribution Theory (RRT)

Real-time redistribution theory (RRT) forms the essential core that enables the data-adjustable structure within DEFT's design framework. RRT establishes a new way of equity interventions through continuous redistribution systems instead of previously used periodic interventions like annual policy assessments and budget adjustments and decennial census updating. According to this theory, equity requires complete alignment with social changes and economic developments and environmental needs and must function automatically in response to emerging inequalities and changing supply and demand levels and crisis circumstances.

According to the RRT, equity operates across national- and system-level boundaries as an interweaving world issue. Every community stands interdependently in its own space and therefore needs transnational collective responsibility to resolve equity issues. As seen in Figure 3.1, RRT presents a recommendation for equity-based interventions to collaborate across international boundaries in order to ensure resources and benefits follow a global approach that recognizes worldwide interconnected systems. RRT promotes the establishment of teamed-up data management systems with international governing structures and worldwide networking capabilities to tackle complex issues involving wellness together with economic problems and environmental problems.

https://doi.org/10.1515/9783112222140-003

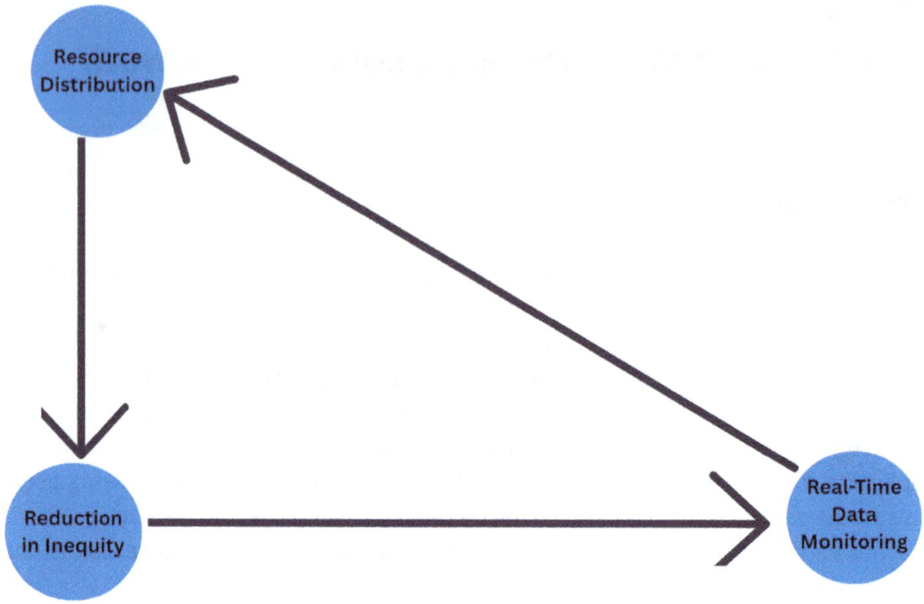

Figure 3.1: RRT system.

Holistic Value Equity Theory (HVET)

Holistic value equity theory (HVET) shows that the equity should not be limited to only financial, rather it is a holistic approach. The HVET explains true equity by introducing various indicators that move from human wellbeing to financial development.

It is anticipated that the theory will keep the social, cultural, economic, and legal determinants of inequal behaviour. The results will shed light on the most successful legislative initiatives that will support equality in all its forms. These evidence-based results will target the identified factors that contribute to the evil by utilizing the main data analysis. As illustrated in Figure 3.2, the purpose of the HVET is to provide policymakers with information on ways to reduce inequality not only economic but also other by identifying the key variables and recommending specific solutions. The results of the study can be used for the creation of more sensible laws and enforcement tactics, which would eventually improve the social wellbeing.

Temporal Equity Shift Theory (TEST)

As per temporal equity shift theory (TEST), the equity changes are constant rather a temporary. As far as the economic factors are concerned, the findings suggest that people's opinions of economic issues have a major impact on how likely they are involved

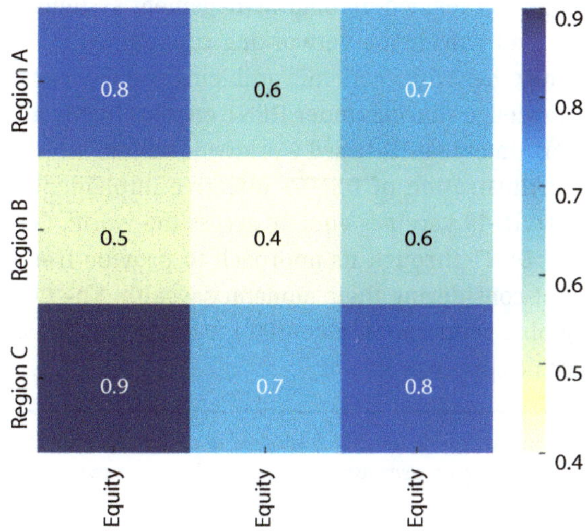

Figure 3.2: Equity heatmap HVET.

in equity. Particularly, as there is a positive relationship between economic factors and the government attitude, individuals have high chances of being unbiased when their economic conditions are better. People engage in tax evasion activities once they find themselves economically safe and secure. The improved financial conditions promote tax evasion as people fear less for the consequences. Such scenario implies that there is importance of compliance strategies and economic conditions that help in making such policies to promote tax compliance. Only well-developed economic conditions are not a solution but the incentives for compliance and making people aware of importance of taxes' contribution for the betterment of the society should be the required solution. Analysing the relationship between economic conditions and crime allows for the development of better interventions to enhance legal compliance. TEST enables equity to exist beyond present circumstances by connecting to both fair historical interpretations and responsible future planning.

Dynamic Equity Network Theory (DENT)

According to the dynamic equity network theory (DENT), equity operates across national- and system-level boundaries as an interweaving world issue. Every community stands interdependently in its own space and therefore needs transnational collective responsibility to resolve equity issues. DENT presents a recommendation for equity-based interventions to collaborate across international boundaries in order to ensure resources and benefits follow a global approach that recognizes worldwide interconnected systems.

DENT promotes the establishment of teamed-up data management systems with international governing structures and worldwide networking capabilities to tackle complex issues involving wellness together with economic problems and environmental problems. The resource and knowledge sharing under DENT enables highly adaptable response measures that support timely needs-based worldwide action.

COVAX serves as an excellent illustration of DENT's effective implementation through its mission to distribute COVID-19 vaccines equally across the world. COVAX demonstrated the core concepts of DENT through its approach to provide free vaccines to developing nations without considering their monetary wealth. The COVAX initiative demonstrates superior global cooperation potential for equity despite dealing with delivery timeline and vaccine supply problems.

FACT: WHO announced that COVAX operation would provide two billion vaccines to countries during 2021 yet high-income nations bought 72% of the initial stock which demonstrates how global equity networks function and what challenges they face.

Algorithmic Governance Equity Theory (AGET)

The algorithmic governance equity theory (AGET) requires built-in support for equity to conduct algorithmic governance procedures in healthcare together with law enforcement and social services. Within the framework of AGET, algorithms need to show clear operations and explain their process to users and undergo permanent assessment for identifying biases that affect disadvantaged communities. The concept protects governing algorithms by requiring equality principles even as it enables algorithmic operations in governance.

The AGET framework specifically applies to criminal justice applications because algorithms play a role in determining sentences and performing parole assessments and risk evaluations. Algorithms have the ability to keep and enhance pre-existing biases in data, which result in the continuous generation of inequality when appropriate safeguards are not in place. The AGET model requires strong oversight mechanisms to perform continuous updates of governance algorithms as well as perform fair audits on their data processing systems.

The implementation of AGET includes regulations that govern the operations of law enforcement facial recognition systems. Legal agencies across multiple jurisdictions must now expose their algorithm accuracy data while providing demographic-based impact analysis to their programmers. Such transparency enables fair use of these technologies according to AGET principles which focus on fairness and accountability.

FACT: Research from NIST dating to 2019 demonstrated facial recognition systems would mistake Asian and Black faces 100 times more often than White faces thus verifying the immediate requirement for algorithmic fairness.

Equity Feedback Loop Theory (EFLT)

According to the equity feedback loop theory (EFLT), equity moves forward as a cycle that relies on consistent input from community members. According to EFLT, the development of equitable policies requires ongoing feedback from the groups that their initiatives seek to help particularly those who face discrimination or have been historically ignored. A feedback system enables both policy implementation and continuous adjustments, which depend on direct experiences of the targeted individuals.

The EFLT system purposes to overturn conventional top-down methods because it believes communities need to fully participate in decisions that shape their future. The approach leads to better solutions which respond directly to the persistent equity gaps of communities.

Participatory budgeting stands out as a practical example of EFLT because this process is currently used in New York and Paris and other cities. The residents of these cities including marginalized communities possess the opportunity to submit project ideas for public funding while also participating in project voting. Through this inclusive mechanism of decision-making, the resources receive allocations that accurately mirror priority needs of the communities most affected by policies thereby enabling live adjustments of equity tools. EFLT improves systems of governance when it merges community suggestions for better accountability and dynamic results.

FACT: The 2021 New York City participatory budgeting process distributed 70% of its funding towards projects from areas previously underserved by the city (NYC Civic Engagement Commission).

Environmental Equity Integration Theory (EEIT)

The environmental equity integration theory (EEIT) states that social equity efforts should integrate with sustainability approaches because these two concepts form interdependent goals. The program suggests that the systems involving eco-friendly mechanisms will guard the weak people from severe environmental disasters and will offer equal access to the natural resources among the different groups of people.

The nature and climate perseverance are ensured by EEIT while inculcating the components such as clean air and drinking water supply. The implementation of EEIT makes sure environmental sustainability becomes essential in accomplishing social and economic equity goals.

Singapore uses its urban planning model as an exemplary implementation of EEIT by uniting environmental data about biodiversity and green structures with socioeconomic measurement tools. The integrated approach guarantees social status is not a barrier to receiving clean air along with parks and climate-resilience measures that support long-term sustainability.

FACT: Black and Latinx communities experience twice the pollution exposure compared to the pollution they generate, while White communities experience disproportionately less than their share of pollution according to research from PNAS (2019).

Predictive Equity Planning Theory (PEPT)

The predictive equity planning theory (PEPT) moves beyond reactive solutions through predictive analytic systems that help anticipate and prevent potential inequities to happen before they fully develop. PEPT depends on the knowledge and data from different sources. It forecasts future conditions where inequities may arise.

The framework of PEPT applies to an economic structure that shows minimal changes in income distribution from 1 year to the next. The gig economy has shifted such assumptions because people commonly alternate between different types of employment and joblessness. The restrictive process of deciding who gets benefits and when they get them fails to recognize the income irregularities of people whose financial patterns are not traditional. Government support programs that include food stamps together with disability benefits and both housing assistance and education subsidies provide essential components of static equity models. The programs establish clear requirements for recipients and allocate resources following their predefined rules. The PEPT aims to give essential support to those in need and establish equality between everyone affected.

Cognitive-Equity Synchronization Theory (CEST)

As per the cognitive-equity synchronization theory (CEST), the equity goals require networks among mental abilities that are basically academic qualifications and technological know-how. As per the theory, there are two major components of social and financial aspects, which are the key to mental ability of individuals. Figure 3.3 offers more explanation with the power access matrix.

CEST is dependent on the schooling abilities of the individuals. It assembles with psychological assistance and digital well-being as these components establish collective communities. The groups that are financially stable tend to have open access to the available resources and they enjoy the perks of the political and economic dominance. They further are receiving the developments in the personal as well as professional sectors.

Low Power	High Power
Low Access to Cognitive Resources	Moderate Access
Moderate Access	High Access to Cognitive Resources

Figure 3.3: Power access matrix CEST.

Conclusion

DEFT comprises basically nine theories to establish its essential framework which offers a much-needed system for the current equity management. The Reflexive Redistribution Theory (RRT) is the foundational core of the DEFT framework that enables its data-adjustable structural integrity. RRT establishes a novel paradigm for equity interventions centered on continuous redistribution systems, which represents a shift from legacy periodic models like annual policy assessments, budget adjustments and decennial census updates. The theory formally posits that genuine equity requires complete functional alignment with emergent social changes, economic developments and environmental needs. RRT is engineered to operate autonomously and continuously. It will activate in direct response to detected emerging inequalities, shifting supply/demand dynamics and crisis circumstances. The Distributed Equity Networking Theory (DENT) mandates the establishment of collaborative data management systems that are designed to be integrated with international governing structures. DENT features worldwide networking capabilities intended to resolve complex, cross-jurisdictional issues of wellness, economic stability and environmental sustainability. On the other hand, the Algorithmic Governance and Equity Theory (AGET) is specialized for criminal justice applications, specifically for cases in which algorithmic models are used for sentence determination, parole assessments, and risk evaluations. AGET identifies that these algorithms have the capacity to retain and amplify preexisting biases, resulting in the perpetuation of systemic inequality if there is a lack of appropriate safeguards. As a consequence, the AGET model mandates robust oversight mechanisms to be put in place for the continuous updating of governing algorithms and the fair, auditable processing of their underlying data systems. The Environmental and Ecological Integrity Theory (EEIT) ensures environmental and climate integrity by integrating critical components that include a guaranteed clean air supply and a potable water supply. The structural implementation of EEIT ensures that environmental sustainability is crucial for the attainment of social and economic equity objectives. The Predictive Equity and Proactivity Theory (PEPT) goes beyond purely reactive solutions by leveraging progressive predictive analytic systems to forecast and forestall possible inequities from fully manifesting and developing within the system. At a very crucial point, we may also use some metrics to assess the DEFT's potential performances.

Chapter 4
Holistic Value Systems – Equity Beyond Economics

Redefining Value in Equity

The outdated systems of equity define "Justice" as financial owning including the wealth, and home ownerships along with academic benefits. The way out to the differences lies in the resource distribution that is obvious. This limited definition of inequality further weakens the concept of equality among the human beings. This mentality has some serious concerns as it creates disturbance and discrimination among the groups of the society and makes people lose their relationships among each other. However, DEFT improves the equity values as it makes together mental well-being and interpersonal networks while promoting long-term development through its amended features.

Equal participation in society leads to its best functioning since emotional health proves fundamental for this process. People lose their ability to engage in education and work and civic life because they do not receive proper trauma treatment in addition to ongoing stress and anxiety. Local challenges do not affect all social groups uniformly. Marginalized communities face increased cumulative stress from systemic barriers because they include racial groups as well as people defined by their gender or social class or disabled individuals and immigrants. The length of time that marginalized communities experience stress directly links to higher chronic illness rates while simultaneously leading to poor academic and employment effects and shorter lifespans according to the American Psychological Association (2019). Equity solutions need to focus on emotional needs because otherwise policies continue to generate harm rather than stopping it.

Social cohesion functions as an essential factor in developing equal societies. Social cohesion refers to the strength of relationships and the degree of solidarity among members of a community. A cohesive community depends on mutual trust together with shared norms and the support members offer one another and the feeling of belonging among members. Statistics from the OECD (2020) establish that social cohesion in communities leads to decreased crime activities and enhanced public health achievements together with increased civic participation. These cohesive communities demonstrate greater ability to withstand diverse crises since economic downturns and natural disasters do not affect them substantially. Community trust building and social fragmentation management are essential elements for equity work because insufficient attention to these factors may create more inequalities than it resolves.

Building infrastructure and housing through urban development has typically been achieved without addressing existing communities or protecting their social connections. Urban projects that change an area's character drive gentrification as the local residents must vacate their homes while their social connections to their com-

https://doi.org/10.1515/9783112222140-004

munity dissolve. Such projects demonstrate limited long-term equity value because they fail to recognize social belonging on the same level as housing units or job placements.

Social and environmental sustainability deserve much more attention as equity components. People neglect how environmental matters relate to social justice while evidence shows their mutual impact. The poor and marginalized populations bear the most environmental degradation because they reside closest to industrial sites like factories together with highways, waste disposal areas and toxic pollution sources. The present communities lack both financial capabilities and enough political influence to combat damaging environmental policies and practices.

Climate change acts as an intensifier of social inequalities because it delivers additional exposure of vulnerable groups to severe weather phenomena and nutrition instability and population displacement and health dangers.

The identification of environmental justice requires standards that integrate equity principles for its framework. The holistic value systems of DEFT identify the basic principles of equity through standards, which define easy and affordable access to clean water and air as well as green spaces with resilient infrastructure. Human dignity together with opportunity exists as a fundamental requirement which sustainability represents according to this perspective.

Individuals' beliefs about social factors have importance on their equity behaviour. As per findings, higher social treatments about the conditions of the people have an increased effect on financial discrepancies. This tells us that how social treatments are crucial in examining such behaviour. Individuals find themselves engaged in these practices if they believe it is easily doable and their society accepts such attitude towards these treatments. If the pressure from peers is lower, the people involve in making discrimination on the basis of colour, race, creed, and gender. This indicated that social influence is powerful enough to shape behaviour related to compliance. How peer group is supposed to behave, how the society perceives about inequality, and how much common it is to do so: all come under social considerations. If the economic difference is normal and acceptable in the society, individuals are less inclined to these concepts. Similarly, if the legal compliance is considered a good and valuable act by the society, people tend to avoid engaging in these things that are biased. In this way, the discrimination can be lowered by bringing changes in the social values and norms about the equality. The legal representatives need to introduce such changes in social attitudes that enhance equality both financially and socially by running public awareness campaigns and community development initiatives. Various worldwide programmes display how a whole-system approach can operate in practice.

Holistic Metrics and Policy Shifts

Through its innovative financial framework, New Zealand illustrates the methods public finance modernizes for the world to observe. The 2019 Wellbeing Budget became a landmark for New Zealand after it established mental health together with child well-being and indigenous equity and environmental sustainability at a similar priority status as traditional economic growth indicators (New Zealand Treasury, 2019). National success is the central reason behind this plan instead of concentrating exclusively on raising national income levels. The practical implementation includes expanding psychotherapy allocations together with child poverty intervention strategies and financial support towards Māori and Pasifika populations who previously received minimal policy consideration.

New Zealand uses the Living Standards Framework which the New Zealand Treasury developed as a policy guidance tool through its 12 connected well-being domains. The system consists of four essential components, which are subjective well-being along with social capital together with cultural identity and environmental stewardship. Real-life data enables authorities to develop governance approaches for promoting inclusive practices through assessment within each domain. The development of metric-based well-being systems in New Zealand has positioned the country among the world leaders in designing policies that include everyone.

The international prestige of Bhutanese territory supports its comprehensive well-being approach through national governance. Bhutan created the Gross National Happiness Index, which functions as both an economic growth indicator challenger and national policy decision platform. GNH serves as the national development assessment system by evaluating nine domains, which include psychological well-being, health, education, time use, cultural diversity, good governance, community vitality, ecological diversity, and living standards.

The economic development standards do not apply to Bhutan since the country acknowledges emotional well-being through spiritual health combined with cultural integration and environmental preservation.

GNH encounters implementation challenges due to its subjective measurement but its basic concepts hold significant importance to the concept as a whole. The nation-building approach of Bhutan provides an effective remedy against reductionist thinking to states seeking a different definition of success. Natural sciences should prioritize happiness sustainability together with collective well-being as their primary evaluation metrics rather than treating them as secondary goals.

Educational systems use total measurement criteria to maintain equivalent academic results across all subjects. The Scottish educational system utilizes the Curriculum for Excellence (CfE) as a useful demonstration. Through its structure, the CfE framework establishes four essential competencies which students must develop covering areas of successful learners along with confident individuals and responsible citizens and effective contributors. The curriculum includes emotional literacy combined with social responsibility and mental well-being at its core to achieve its mission. There exist two types of assessments in teaching which combine academic performance assessment alongside social and emotional student development indicators (Scottish Government, 2021).

The Scottish government shows recognition that students must achieve full potential through both emotional resilience and psychological safety. Several well-being assessment measurements together with self-evaluation instruments and community development activities in schools promote better student participation and fewer school incidents and stronger educator-student bonds.

Numerous nations worldwide implement the same educational approaches in their learning institutions. The Finnish educational system gives well-being priority because the national perspective was established years back. Educators learn social-teaching methods and schools adopt welcoming zones with designed stress-reducing features. Success within Finnish education approaches education as a partnership between students and teachers and supports environments through minimal standard examination obligations. The design choices made in Finnish schools have led to high education ranking positions and an enhancement of student satisfaction while yielding better mental health outcomes.

The private business sector increasingly focuses on this direction of transformation. The operations of businesses incorporate environmental social and governance (ESG) metrics using a triple bottom line accounting system for success assessment, which evaluates profit together with people and planet aspects. Social entrepreneurship and impact investing operate as new profitable industries to measure financial returns and validated social impacts. The indicators demonstrate how organizations redefine value measurement to exceed financial gains for shareholders.

There are plenty of nations that are getting it into practice the welfare and improving the social health by collaborating the moral values and long-term merits. The fast-paced increasing climate problems and disunity among various groups on the earth along with psychological disorders encourage the concerned to create straight relation among the financial, human, and environmental objectives. A thorough and the entire concept in the systemic structure is an amazing recipe to the ensure equality in all its forms.

The strategies discussed in this paper detail the implementation methods for these principles within healthcare organizations and education structures and housing construction plans and climate control frameworks.

Case Study: Mental Health Initiatives in Schools

Finland: Mental Health Education as Curriculum

Popular beliefs contradict the fact that Finnish educational reform remains well known yet their school system avoids clear mental health interventions. Primary school Finnish educational curricula provide formal instruction regarding managing stress and emotional control as well as interpersonal competency training and anxiety recognition ability development. The lessons operate at the same time as standard academic curriculum subjects.

Every school in Finland can utilize allocated funds to obtain onsite mental health services. Every educational facility in Finland needs to have mental health nurses together with counselors and special education staff who work with teachers and families. The combined presence of these specialists constitutes a compulsory requirement. Education organizations introduce peer-mentoring programs to develop student networks that support emotional needs of fellow students.

The model finds acceptance from present educational guidelines which administer the nation. The educational system educates about mental health in a structured manner while simultaneously allocating resources and conducting assessments regarding these initiatives. The educational aspect exists distinctively outside of teaching staff requirements and responsibilities. The Finnish National Agency for Education performs standard evaluations to assess both student welfare programs and learning facilities.

The impact is striking. The strong performance of Finnish students in PISA (Programme for International Student Assessment) measurements continues despite the Finnish education system never enforcing standardized test requirements. Finland-based students demonstrate high levels of motivation along with low stress levels compared to students who follow education systems based on pressure. Research by Pasi Sahlberg (2015) supports the well-being initiative which shows its ability to produce long-term academic accomplishment. Finland's dedication to excellent mental health principles has transformed how to establish high-performing settings with equal opportunities for all students.

Canada: The School Mental Health ASSIST Model in Ontario

Since 2011 the "School Mental Health ASSIST" began working in Ontario as the provincial support organization to help school boards execute mental health promotion and prevention along with intervention services for K-12 students.

The main strategy behind this initiative concentrates on giving both educators and school administrators the proper knowledge base and functional capabilities. A comprehensive professional development program teaches personnel to detect first indicators of mental disturbances while also enabling them to use research-backed interventions for mental health support in classrooms. School mental health responsibilities in Ontario extend from education institution to education organization thus integrating mental health into regular student activities beyond separating guidance responsibilities.

The structured intervention approaches within School Mental Health ASSIST support the core aspects of its program design. The promotion strategies focus on classroom mindfulness exercises and school-wide wellness programs operate as part of a system that provides additional support to students with moderate symptoms and intensive interventions for students with complex needs. Schools can customize the framework according to their specific population and obstacles since the framework is adaptable and adjustable.

A research study by Kutcher et al. (2016) produced statistically significant positive outcomes regarding behavioral incidents throughout schools implementing the initiative. Students who participated in the intervention developed better learning participation skills and showed improved personal well-being results. The data collected from evaluations proves the success of mental health integration in schools as it proves the approach works effectively to reduce educational gaps between students.

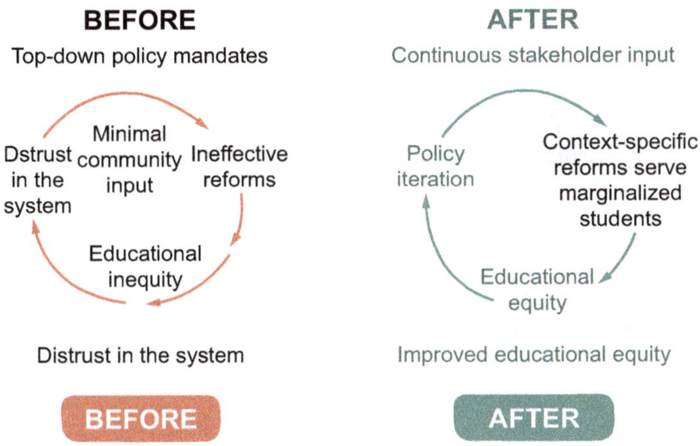

Figure 4.1: Comparison.

Linking Policy to Equity

Mental health initiatives rise above being basic health interventions because they function as equality-promoting tools according to the experiences of Finland and Ontario. The children from underserved communities face many problems caused by insufficient wealth and ethnic bias and unstable domestic conditions. The implementation of system-wide emotional and psychological resilience initiatives defends students from negative consequences of multiple stress factors by allowing uninterrupted development both academically and socially. Figure 4.1 is a comparison of the process before and after the implementation.

Community Cohesion and Policy Innovation

The law has no ability to create community cohesion; rather a robust and efficient framework with the amendments that are culturally suitable with the norms and values of the people supports the integrity among the divided groups. The dynamic equity framework theory (DEFT) considers social togetherness as one of the most important factors to produce equity. The integration among the people is a sign of combined willpower to make stronger groups and put efforts together.

Superblocks represent small urban regeneration sites with child-friendly play spaces as well as shaded areas where neighbours organically socialize. The Barcelona City Council (2019) shows renovated areas generate increased human foot traffic and better air quality in the area.

The implementation of Superblocks proves to be strong social infrastructure components that deliver additional environmental advantages. The initiative accomplishes urban restructuring which gives higher priority to people instead of vehicles while simultaneously creating communal bonds between residents. The local community members feel safer because the area has encouraged stronger connections with neighbours and residents actively participate in community-based events. The initiative enables architectural constructs by welcoming citizens to actively engage with civic initiatives.

Such changes transcend mere surface-level appearances because they affect equity levels in the community. Historically, many low-income residential areas have faced problems such as inadequate investment and both intentional and environmental neglect. The city possesses insufficient parks while its sidewalks remain in poor condition and navigational traffic arrangements usually support distant communal movements instead of supporting neighbourhood functioning. Superblocks actively work to reorganize public facilities in space while closing gaps that affect community health and social connections. The planning process enhances physical conditions and gives marginalized communities a sense of empowerment because it shows that their neighbourhoods deserve vital attention and care.

Social relationships among citizens form a necessary condition for fair development despite widespread distributed value to this element. According to Putnam (2000), high social capital leads to better civic engagement, supports stronger economies, and minimizes crime while improving public health results (Putnam, 2000). The design of social spaces in urban areas through policy initiatives directly aids the development of this resource.

Major cities throughout the world have established policy measures that strengthen social connections between residents. Seoul implements the "Sharing City" initiative through communal services that provide shared childcare and tool libraries and co-housing programmes which strengthen collective community resilience. These services minimize individual expenses through improved interdependence and mutual aid which acts as an equity multiplier in increasing precarious conditions.

Medellín Colombia implemented social urbanism as its solution to combat violence by developing a system employing escalators and cable cars together with educational and cultural projects to restore cut off neighbourhoods. The projects function to achieve two goals by transporting individuals through distances and restoring social cohesion while rebuilding civic unity.

Policy recognition of different cultures functions as an essential key to achieve cohesion. Administrative policies that appreciate and honour different social communities within a community space create stronger feelings of belongingness among its members. Inclusive societies form through providing language services and indigenous governing framework backing together with multicultural art installations that enable community members to see reflections of themselves with respect. Public policy demonstrates either alienation between citizens through deficient design or creation of political solidarity through its implementation.

The development of cohesive policies needs to adopt an adaptable approach. The success formula in Barcelona fails to reproduce identical results outside its territory. Adapted governance systems combined with functional testing methods along with local testing areas represent essential elements. From DEFT's viewpoint, adaptive models should be used because community cohesion exists as an active process adapting to population changes and social conflicts and natural environmental factors.

Digital tools serve as amplification means for cohesion efforts if used properly. Notwithstanding the need to protect digital inclusion we should exercise special care because marginalized communities need both equitable access to technology and proper training to use digital equipment successfully.

The development of cohesive communities stands as a real policy-based solution for creating balanced societies. The combination of relational infrastructure which Barcelona showcases through its Superblocks system and other global implementations creates sustainable fairness because cities understand economic expansion requires both measures. DEFT acknowledges that policy transformations centre these innovations because effective communities form the basis of complete justice.

Environmental Equity as a Holistic Component

FACT: The Environmental Protection Agency demonstrates through reporting that Latino communities face triple exposure rates to nitrogen dioxide in comparison to white communities.

Equity needs the essential element of environmental justice to become a complete equitable system. People who live in marginalized areas bear most of the burden from environmental destruction despite having no power in forming ecological policies. According to the Environmental Protection Agency (EPA), residents of colour within the US communities face exposure to particulate matter that exceeds white communities by 50% in statistics.

As the DEFT demonstrates, environmental justice needs to become a foundation in all equity structures. The method acknowledges social inequalities in environmental damage and climate exposure require equal attention because they form the foundation of true social justice.

Medellín's Green Corridors: A Model for Environmental Equity

Modern environmental equity finds an excellent example in Medellin Colombia's "Green Corridors" project. The programme started in 2016 to produce a 20-km green network by connecting 18 roads and 12 waterways into 1 integrated green space. The project established its purpose to control increasing urban heat along with improving air quality while focusing on underserved communities. Figure 4.2 reflects the advantages of ensuring environmental justice.

Figure 4.2: Diagram loop.

This urban initiative has produced major positive outcomes in its deployment. Studies showed that the average temperature in the city decreased by 2°C while surface temperatures dropped by 10.3°C in targeted areas. The implementation of the project delivered better air quality alongside community gathering areas which helped boost community health alongside social bond between residents.

The Green Corridors project delivered additional social and economic advantages in addition to environmental advantages. The city paid employment and skills training to 75 citizens with disadvantaged backgrounds who became certified city gardeners and planting technicians. The project shows how environmental and societal improvement work together towards a comprehensive perspective which DEFT endorses.

Integrating Environmental Justice into Policy

Medellin's green project indicates how the environmental stuff be put forward in the policy formulation. Cities achieve social equity through their dedication to install green infrastructure systems in communities with limited resources.

The Environmental Protection Agency maintains two tools like EJScreen and EnviroAtlas to detect the communities facing elevated exposure to environmental hazards within the United States. Policy tools present powerful capabilities that allow decision-makers to use data for directing funds and making decisions towards environmental justice priorities.

Active involvement of community members should be central during the process of creating and executing environmental policies. Community involvement within policy decisions enables environmental measures to match the requirements and essential needs of people who face environmental impacts. People who take part in such collaborative efforts establish better trust levels and raise accountability while producing enduring solutions.

The framework of holistic equity requires environmental equity to be as essential as its other components. Environmental justice requires two main strategies – combining environmental policies with justice principles and involving local communities in choosing development decisions. Additionally, disadvantaged regions should receive investments for green systems.

Towards Multidimensional Equity Models

Equity achieves true adaptability when its definition incorporates both elaborate and all-encompassing contents. The material exchange of money cannot be the sole interpretation of equity. The basic elements of housing and education alongside income and employment deliver substantial value to equity but these essential components fail to explain the complete justice framework of society. Elements establish human survival capacities in individual lives and community organizational systems that drive long-term social standards across multiple generations.

International governments have ignored these non-economic indicators which they define as "soft metrics" since they failed to consider them during budget allocations and urban plan development and institutional reforms for numerous years.

Conclusion

Therefore, DEFT provides a blueprint to the limited equity concept by adding justice aspects in its thorough framework. Besides it, social and environmental sustainability deserve much more attention as equity components. People neglect how environmental matters relate to social justice while evidence shows their mutual impact. The poor and marginalized populations bear the most environmental degradation because they reside closest to industrial sites like factories together with highways, waste disposal areas, and toxic pollution sources. The present communities lack both financial capabilities and enough political influence to combat damaging environmental policies and practices.

This section investigates institutional reform processes which seek to reconstruct schools and healthcare systems and city councils according to DEFT's multidimensional standards. Damaging automated systems that form public life will be addressed by creating new methodologies for building fair explainable algorithms. Participatory governance will teach us to give communities the power to help build the governing systems they will live under.

Our effort to redefine valued aspects changes far more than our measurement techniques because it reimages the future. The future should consider success beyond mere GDP measurements by promoting synergistic progress among people and their natural surroundings and innovative thought. Such a future establishes equity as an active system that uses dignity and inclusion with sustainability to ensure continuous development.

Chapter 5
Real-World Applications and Case Studies

Introduction

The main purpose of this chapter exists to connect theoretical concepts with practical use by showing how dynamic equity framework theory (DEFT) operates across different real-world applications. This chapter applies theoretical principles established in previous sections by creating achievable solutions based on DEFT. The book offers multiple focused case analyses within healthcare services and education systems and environmental policy as well as automated system management, which demonstrate the practical value of implementing DEFT principles to enhance both organizational decision systems and resource allocation and equality results. For each instance our experts selected we observed how DEFT works when institutions include it into their frameworks. This chapter demonstrates the functional use of DEFT through sector-specific examples so it can establish itself as an operational tool for creating justice-centred and data-driven inclusive systems that benefit both the public and private domains.

Healthcare: AI-Based Resource Allocation in Hospitals

FACT: CDC (2021) reported that near half of U.S. rural hospital COVID-19 deaths stemmed from a lack of available resources whereas Italian ICU bed availability rates differed by as much as 70% between regions during the pandemic. IBM's Watson AI operational model would have allocated healthcare resources in real time to save thousands of people from avoidable mortality according to JAMA (2021).

Systemic inefficiencies within healthcare have persistently affected the distribution of medical resources since they primarily disrupted healthcare equity. Healthcare institutions face intensified challenges to resource efficiency during health crises because their traditional distribution systems (based on fixed quotas and census models and historical usage data) cannot operate effectively in response to increased care requirements. The real-time redistribution theory (RRT) serves as a vital part of DEFT through its implementation of functions that make resource adjustments based on real-time data changes.

https://doi.org/10.1515/9783112222140-005

The Problem of Static Allocation in Health Systems

Standard healthcare systems depend on allocation strategies that do not change. Hospitals together with clinics base their supply distribution on projected need patterns and historical records and administrative policy requirements. The administration-friendly approach of these models does not work effectively with sudden changes in population distribution or localized outbreaks or systemic inequalities that exist in geographic and income zones.

Health systems displayed a stubborn refusal to adapt when COVID-19 struck healthcare facilities around the world. The worldwide health system together with those in population-rich areas faced critical failure due to an excessive surge in patient demand. Inadequate fast reaction to moving hotspots caused major problems especially among disadvantaged groups.

Case Study: COVID-19 Response in Italy and the United States

The pandemic arrived in Italy during early 2020 to become Europe's first impact point resulting in Lombardy's hospitals reaching their safe bed occupancy capacity in the ICU. The research conducted by Grasselli et al. (JAMA, 2020) demonstrated how connectivity problems prevented hospitals with unused resources from helping facilities with severe ventilator and staff shortages.

During the first pandemic wave, New York and Detroit faced severe medical shortages but rural healthcare facilities in other areas maintained lower levels of patient care needs. An examination of medical resource distribution by McKinsey & Company (2020) and other health policy organizations showed AI-assisted tools would have directed Personal Protective Equipment along with ICU beds and medical staff with higher efficiency and fairness to save numerous lives.

The Real-Time Redistribution Theory (RRT) from DEFT provides the foundation for this Application

Through RRT artificial intelligence and machine learning technologies function together to detect emerging patterns while forecasting healthcare needs to both specify resource shifts and perform them as needed. Equity functions under RRT as an ongoing goal that gets regularly assessed and updated during its continuous operation. Key principles of RRT include the following:

1. Health networks supply continuous data streams of patient admissions and disease spread alongside emergency call information as well as ICU capacity and diagnostic examination numbers for instant analysis.

2. AI systems produce simulated future scenarios that depend on present-time trends which enables healthcare organizations to develop surge-preparedness strategies in advance.
3. RRT guides proactive resource movement involving ventilators along with staff members and vaccines to locations with high-risk levels identified by the model.

Through cross-evaluative coordination, this system positions healthcare facilities to coordinate with regional health systems rather than operating in isolation.

Equity in Action: Prioritizing the Most Vulnerable

The RRT operated by DEFT intentionally allocates resources with priority given towards people who have historically faced limited care. Rural as well as low-income urban hospitals face restricted access to political attention and financial resources that equal those of metropolitan medical institutions. Resources under a DEFT-guided system serve two critical functions: achieving operational efficiency along with formulating remedies to overturn historical discrepancies.

The predictive models using AI system guidance from DEFT would consider social vulnerability scores combined with area poverty rates and assess previous funding inequalities. The occurrence of a similar number of cases in low-income areas with poor baseline infrastructure would lead to an enhanced public health response than what would be deployed in upper-income areas with stronger baseline capabilities.

The system embeds these metrics into real-time decision systems as a part of its framework while drawing from Social Vulnerability Index approaches but extends its application by integrating these metrics for dynamic decision-making systems. Figure 5.1 shows the process of applying DEFT in healthcare.

Implementation Architecture

To achieve success with healthcare AI employing DEFT requires installation of following elements:

1. ***Interoperable Data Infrastructure***
   Hospitals together with clinics labs and emergency services need to provide standardized data to one common system. The system requirement includes electronic health records (EHRs) along with laboratory results as well as inventory counts and human resource capacity information.
2. ***Transparent Algorithms***
   Black-box systems produce no possibility of reaching fairness goals. The algorithms need explanation capabilities while being submitted to regular bias evalu-

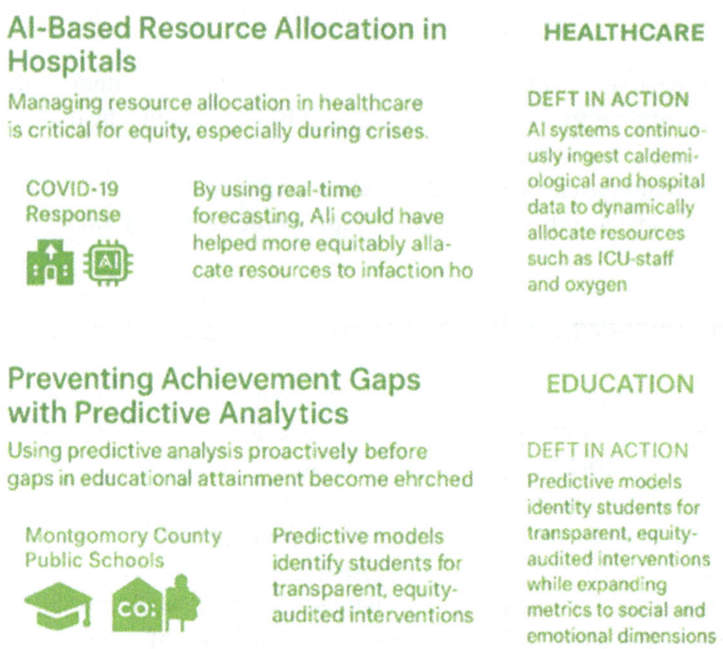

Figure 5.1: Applications of DEFT.

ations which embody the principles of algorithmic governance equity theory (AGET as presented in Chapter 2.

3. ***Decentralized but Synchronized Governance***
   The system needs to support coordinated interventions across facilities even though each hospital region operates independently. According to the dynamic equity network theory (DENT) health equity operates as a regional and often transnational matter that requires coordination.
4. ***Ethical Oversight Committees***
   Human-supervised models protect ethical principles specifically in cases of important triage processes and critical resource movement decisions.

Success Story: AI Resource Allocation Pilot in the United Kingdom

Machine learning tools entered service with the UK National Health Service (NHS) when the COVID-19 pandemic progressed to its later stages for predicting critical care unit admissions and resource requirements. Medical personnel in London employed real-time hospital information to direct ambulances properly while readjusting employee shifts and moving hospital resources. The experimental program run by NHS Digital achieved a 18% decrease in ICU beds being empty as well as improving emergency room wait times by 22%.

This pilot demonstrates how AI-driven redistribution systems fulfil the core principles of DEFT even though the pilot was not specifically derived from DEFT concepts. These models have the potential to develop into definitive DEFT-aligned health system networks with the implementation of specific equity performance metrics.

The movement from crisis management towards standard healthcare operations constitutes the path ahead. The original purpose of RRT emerged from crisis situations, yet its future applications extend towards daily medical operation management. For example:

1. AI technology utilizes predictive capabilities to foresee flu season demands thus it controls resources of vaccines alongside testing materials.
2. The analysis of real-time data allows healthcare personnel to detect unserved communities where diabetes and heart disease are on the rise to initiate specific population-based actions.

Conclusion: Equity at the Speed of Data

The equity of healthcare based on information should happen, so as we do not look for semi or annually reports. The current health system should be supporting the existing forms of the reality. The healthcare sector can be enhanced by regulating the RTR theory of DEFT.

As the health issues are increasing day by day, the DEFT should be involved in the system to carry out necessary actions and resolve with the help of AI.

Education: Preventing Achievement Gaps with Predictive Analytics

The most important and pressing issue of education poses great threats to the world. It continues to disturb the world as it could not handle it yet efficiently and effectively. The previous results show that the system relied on outdated stuff that caused lot of damage to the system. These measures provide outcome data about students but they cannot detect warning signs that will affect future educational differences. These measurements assess gaps in achievement only after they expand so they provide no practical assistance for developing preventive interventions.

The predictive equity planning theory (PEPT) within the DEFT addresses this critical shortfall. PEPT supports using predictive analytics for antecedent threat identification of inequality rather than it supports maintaining existing social inequalities.

PEPT uses responsible data application to move educational equity from reactive policy towards proactive prevention.

FACT: U.S. public school students who were Latino and Black experienced learning loss during COVID-19 at rates four to five times higher than their White peers which indicates an immediate requirement for predictive systems similar to the early-warning system in Montgomery County that decreased dropout risks by more than thirty percent (McKinsey, 2021).

The Limits of Traditional Educational Metrics

Standard educational systems use end-of-year test scores together with GPA results and standardized assessments whenever they measure student achievement while distributing resources. Retrospective assessment tools hold limited value in understanding the comprehensive behavioural patterns affecting students particularly from different minority backgrounds. A student dealing with housing issues coupled with caregiving duties and unmanaged mental health concerns does not display instant test score declines yet the ongoing stressor can compel them to leave school.

The observations show signs of insufficient support systems rather than deficient abilities of students. PEPT solves this problem through its utilization of predictive tracking data, which detects warning signs of learning loss and vulnerability before standardized assessment methods become active.

Case Study: Montgomery County Public Schools, Maryland

The education sector of Maryland benefits from Montgomery County Public Schools (MCPS), which leads predictive analytics work in the field. Furthermore, while vast research exists on DEFT, there is indeed a lack of empirical and theoretical literature through which either individual aspects of schools or a combination of various factors is analysed holistically with respect to economic, social, cultural, and legal dimensions in Montgomery County Public Schools, Maryland. The authors recognize that this is an area that has not been investigated in this comprehensive manner; this study seeks to fill this gap by exploring the multiple links of the specified variables and consequently the overall effects on DEFT conduct. It is in this regard that this research will endeavour to include primary data in an effort to produce accurate policy interventions for the enhancement of the policy compliance. The results of this research should be beneficial to the relevant authorities and policy makers as they provide an opportunity to understand gaps and invent better approaches to eliminate the problems of education.

DEFT in Action: Ethical and Holistic Predictive Interventions

The organization of equity sets PEPT apart from other systems in entire predictive system. The use of such analytics further operates on the basis of three major theories which helps its operational stuff.

Algorithmic Governance Equity Theory (AGET)

The governance management is one of the most pressing global issues that reduces government revenue and public trust in the system. Using fundamental theories, the DEFT examines the economic, social, cultural, and legal factors of this scenario. The research investigates how different factors such as income levels, employment status, education, social norms, cultural values, and perceptions influence the behaviour towards the governance, as illustrated in Figure 5.2. By AGET, using models the fairness and transparency is ensured as it builds trust and friendly relationships of the public with the governing bodies. Furthermore, the models maintain their accountability that helps in winning the hearts of the common men.

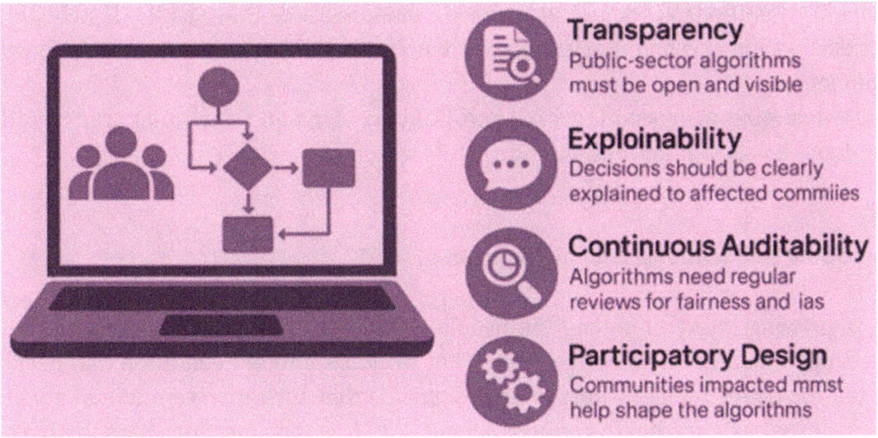

Figure 5.2: Implementing AGET.

The people perceive legal system better and public-oriented when it is equitable, efficient, and strict. Individuals are likely to evade taxes when they are sure about the weaknesses of the legal system that is the system is corrupt, unfair, and unjust. In addition, individuals believe tax evasion is some sort of resistance to unfair and complicated tax systems. While if the legal system is effective, fair, and just, individuals are more likely to build trust in the government and show interest in compliance.

Equity-Focused Learning Theory (EFLT)

The system demands collaboration between the academicians and the students along with their respective families. The audience involvement in the governing body develops a sense of responsibility and trust building that is very core for both the government and the public.

The school must conduct joint consultations with families and students before making adjustments to students who receive attention from predictive models. The approach builds trust while enabling community members to add relevant details which maintains the empowering character and the non-punitive nature of interventions.

Holistic Value Equity Theory (HVET)

PEPT under DEFT significantly increases the educational value metrics since it moves beyond assessing solely cognitive performance data. Hotentots provide an expanded perspective, which includes psychological well-being as well as peer associations and creative abilities and cultural roots within its forecasting system. A comprehensive assessment of student academic progression demonstrates that academic achievement exists within the boundaries of their emotional development as well as social environment.

Both declining peer relationships and bullying signs and declining grades will trigger equal levels of intervention under PEPT systems.

International Implications: Global Adoption of PEPT

There is growing interests among the people globally in PEPT as it happened in the United Kingdom and some other countries. For instance, another condition that needs to be met for policy interventions to be designed is that such interventions in a way must be viewed as effective to counter tax evasion. It is the assertion that when taxpayers find that a policy measure is sound, equitable, and being applied uniformly, they are granted compliance with tax policies. Possible policy measures include reduction and improvement of the tax administration, conducting campaigns that would raise awareness of citizens On the virtues of reporting tax evasion. This is the way the people globally need to be got in touch under PEPT framework of DEFT.

Future Horizons: AI Tutors, Personalized Learning, and Social Equity

The PEPT is also helpful in establishing AI tutoring forums. Consequently, it is for this reason that policies that are implemented to address tax evasion must be adapted sufficiently in a way that they tackle all the mentioned influences. This involves matters such as offering incentives to ensure compliance, changing the perception towards the issue, balanced approach that does not offend courtesy legal changes, and effective policies. The PEPT instruments stress on providing quality educations to the students across the globe who previously have been deprived of quality education.

Besides, the individuals from humble family background with lower incomes can also have access to the prestigious education which in past has been a dream for many. Thus, PEPT is a life-changing theme of the DEFT.

Conclusion: Equity Begins with Foresight

There is growing interests among the people globally in PEPT as it happened in the United Kingdom and some other countries. This involves matters such as offering incentives to ensure compliance, changing the perception towards the issue, balanced approach that does not offend courtesy legal changes, and effective policies. The PEPT instruments stress on providing quality educations to the students across the globe who previously have been deprived of quality education. This is the way the people globally need to be got in touch under PEPT framework of DEFT. The students from humble family background with lower incomes can also have access to the prestigious education which in past has been a dream for many. Thus, PEPT is a life-changing theme of the DEFT.

Climate Change: Managing Carbon Credits with Environmental Equity Integration Theory (EEIT)

Global South marginalized communities experience most of the climate disruption risks that stem from the primary emission sources of industrial nations and international corporations. The shift towards environmentally friendly economic systems has produced mainly benefits for individuals who possess financial resources along with robust infrastructure enabling them to exploit renewable innovations and sustainable farming techniques and carbon schemes.

Numerous climate initiatives fail because they generate the same systemic inequalities that they were intended to eliminate through their asymmetrical nature of effects and causes. EEIT that operates under DEFT directly solves this contradiction. EEIT advocates for significant system redesign of carbon credit markets that will accomplish fair distribution of environmental advantages and burdens and automatic modifications based on community needs.

FACT: Together with UNEP (2022) explains that marginalized populations obtain less than 10% of global climate finance although they experience 80% of climate-induced damages. The carbon market tends to avoid indigenous environmental leaders in countries like Kenya until equity protection measures adopted from DEFT's EEIT framework are implemented.

The concept of carbon credits along with their distribution issues needs thorough understanding

The holder of carbon credits obtains authorization through traded certificates to release specific amounts of carbon dioxide alongside other greenhouse gases. A ton of reduced or avoided emissions leads to an equivalent credit issuance. Carbon credits form part of the trading system where government entities and corporate entities acquire them to both fulfil environmental criteria and minimize their greenhouse gas impact.

The Environmental Protection Agency maintains two tools like EJScreen and EnviroAtlas to detect the communities facing elevated exposure to environmental hazards within the United States. Policy tools present powerful capabilities which allow decision-makers to use data for directing funds and making decisions towards environmental justice priorities. Active involvement of community members should be central during the process of creating and executing environmental policies. Community involvement within policy decisions enables environmental measures to match the requirements and essential needs of people who face environmental impacts. People who take part in such collaborative efforts establish better trust levels and raise accountability while producing enduring solutions. The framework of holistic equity requires environmental equity to be as essential as its other components. Environmental justice requires two main strategies – combining environmental policies with justice principles and involving local communities in choosing development decisions. Additionally, disadvantaged regions should receive investments for green systems.

Case Study: Kenya's Carbon Trading and REDD+ Programs

The REDD+ depicts that how the country responds to the possible merits and demerits by its due contribution. By these projects, the native and living there people receive amounts as income from saving of forests where they sell carbon globally. The consequences are way better as they promote sustainability by conserving forests, catching emissions of carbon and paying the locals of the nation.

There are some roadblocks in the way of making this policy happen as per some international reports that some non-governmental organizations are being imposed and they gain the benefits arising from this project. As a result, indigenous communities – particularly those lacking formal land titles or legal representation – receive only a fraction of the revenues. These communities received no proper understanding about the actual market value of the credits sold because they lacked the power to negotiate fair terms.

The situation demonstrates an ongoing pattern where markets lacking equity protection mechanisms enable the powerful to control financial benefits even though the vulnerable groups store carbon.

DEFT in Action: Integrating EEIT for Climate Justice

The environmental equity integration theory (EEIT) delivers an intelligent solution for this issue. EEIT establishes dynamic equity algorithms to modify carbon credit values through various justice-oriented factors.

TEST exists as the time-focused framework of DEFT, which enables the assessment of both historical unfairness and modern life vulnerabilities. The testing method used by TEST examines each carbon credit on quantitative aspects plus qualitative factors consisting of:

1. Human Development Index (HDI) of the stewarding community
2. Climate risk index of the region
3. Historical exploitation or marginalization of the land and its people
4. Ecological co-benefits such as biodiversity, water retention, or indigenous knowledge
5. Community governance structures and transparency

A carbon offset project run by indigenous people with low HDI and high climate risk would result in a price increase of its carbon credits through the carbon market multipliers. The value of a commercial forest ton in an economically developed nation with modern infrastructure will typically be assessed at its basic rate in the market.

The system functions by praising protection practices while recognizing structural inequalities that creates resilience to climate change in most affected regions.

Technological Tools: Transparent and Decentralized Verification

An effective implementation of EEIT depends on maintaining trust and developing methods for tracking everything. DEFT relies on blockchain-based transparent tracking platforms that display all carbon credit processes from start to finish for each stakeholder.

Such platforms can include:

1. Fund disbursement happens automatically through smart contracts when verification standards get satisfied
2. Equity-adjusted credit value together with its data explanation can be found on public dashboards.
3. Local stakeholders gain access to governance nodes which allow them to participate in voting about project parameters together with data validation activities

Through these tools communities gain full visibility which establishes their ability to regain authority over climate disruption effects that mostly affect them. The local groups have the power to manage their own monitoring functions so cultural expertise can influence how they define carbon values. EEIT seeks growth through regulatory and market-based approaches for expansion.

EEIT needs transitioning regulatory frameworks and the development of global market mechanisms for its global adoption. Key policy levers include:

1. Government entities and multinational corporations must provide superior prices along with tax incentives to purchase credits verified according to principles of EEIT. Justice-based offsets become more desirable within the market through such policy initiatives.
2. International certification organizations including Verra and the UNFCCC along with the Gold Standard need to include justice-oriented metrics into their certification systems that extend past just emission reduction measurements.
3. Local populations must have direct authority in every financial or monitoring phase of carbon projects that generate benefits from their territory.

EEIT completes its architecture with equity principles to avoid exploitation and make sure climate mitigation stands with climate justice.

EEIT Beyond Forests: Urban and Coastal Applications

The discussion about carbon credits usually centres on forest conservation but EEIT can effectively work within urban areas and coastal sites. For example:

1. Upland slums become eligible for carbon credit monetization when rooftop gardens or solar grids are installed and they generate climate savings that should be distributed equally to their residents.
2. Credits from mangrove restoration projects in coastal areas should apply weights to their value according to climate sensitivity and ecosystem biodiversity value improvements.

These applications increase carbon financial opportunities outside rural forests, which allows climate equity to reach every climate response domain.

Conclusion: A Justice-Centred Climate Economy

The events of the climate crisis will shape the twenty-first century alongside the selection process of who receives advantages from climate solutions. EEIT is powerful enough to make carbon credit markets into financial mechanisms that practice climate justice within DEFT. EEIT creates equity metrics using decentralized verification options, which focus on prioritizing vulnerable areas to achieve environmental policy compliance with moral grounds.

The world will succeed in emission reductions and human protections only through carbon accounting that presents more than numerical data but also tells stories. This analysis recognizes both the objects of sequestration along with the actors involved in sequestration processes along with their operational conditions and achieved consequences.

EEIT represents a climate response method that measures the impacts on human populations instead of traditional carbon metric systems.

Governance: Using Algorithmic Governance Equity Theory (AGET) for Transparent Policymaking

FACT: Without the AGET principles embedded in algorithms the SyRI scandal targeted marginalized low-income immigrants resulting in 96% flagging (Human Rights Watch, 2020).

Governments throughout the world implement increasing numbers of algorithmic systems to run public administration tasks and make resource distribution decisions while carrying out governmental rules and regulations. Algorithmic technologies now monitor various public tasks including police operations and the identification of welfare beneficiaries up to immigration screening and automatic tax fraud identification systems. The substantial adoption of algorithmic governance faces increasing opposition because of alleged transparency issues together with discrimination and decreased accountability.

DTFT contains its core element called AGET, which serves as its fundamental construct. AGET establishes an ethical foundation for digital governance because it aims to reprogram algorithms for delivering inclusive fairness while pursuing justice for all members of society.

The Risks of Algorithmic Governance Without Equity

Algorithmic systems gain their knowledge from historical datasets that normally include societal prejudices together with systemic social inequalities. Systems deployed without ethical restrictions develop the potential to create significant discriminatory automation. Taking into account the economic, social, cultural, legal, and policy aspects, it is possible to develop an effective governmental strategy for making reasonable and ethically sound individuals. Such an approach is crucial as part of the overall efforts to improve the operation of the systems and the usability of resulting revenues for well-being of the public. In conclusion, promoting the ethos of compliance together with strengthening the people's confidence in the system will go a long way in helping to build a more informed systems and society.

AGET functions specifically as follows:

1. Transparency

All algorithmic systems deployed in public governance operations need to exhibit transparency under AGET requirements. This includes:

1. *The public disclosure of usable source codes becomes necessary whenever technology permits such action so researchers and civil society and watchdog groups can verify algorithm functions.*
2. *All details about assumptions together with model parameters and training data roots along with decision-making rules should be documented in language that normal people can understand.*

Operating transparently with algorithmic systems makes them easier to understand by multiple actors who can verify their fair performance independently.

2. Explainability

Every decision based on public algorithms should be understandable by both experts and typical citizens. Explainability involves:

1. *People whose lives are affected by algorithmic decisions need to understand precisely why specific outcomes were determined.*
2. *The public needs effective methods to request official evaluations of algorithmically generated decisions through both legal and administrative channels.*
3. *Public explanations need to exist in different languages together with suitable formats that match different community needs.*

The requirement for explainability in the digital realm brings human touch while maintaining court procedure protections.

3. Continuous Auditability

Running algorithms as a fully automated operation without human maintenance is never possible. AGET requires ongoing evaluation through:

1. *Organization conduct equity audits by monitoring algorithmic results through disaggregated assessments of racial and gendered and income-based and geographical and able-bodied communities.*
2. *The surveillance of algorithms needs to detect biased outcomes so that the systems get retrained or become obsolete upon identifying unfair results.*
3. *Third-party institutions such as ethicists along with statisticians and human rights advocates need oversight rights regarding algorithm usage.*

4. Participatory Design

This involves:

1. *System deployment requires ethical impact assessments through which stakeholders combine forces to detect possible harms followed by the formulation of mitigation methods.*
2. *The system needs built-in continuous user feedback processes which enable both real-time system amendments and corrections based on user responses.*

The involvement of users in technology development enables democratic structures of technology development while making algorithms operate within what people actually experience daily.

AGET in Action: Beyond Welfare and Policing

The principles of AGET demonstrate suitable applicability for detecting welfare fraud as well as other governance domains. Consider the following use cases:

1. AI exists to anticipate homelessness situations and allow authorities to establish housing assistance ahead of time. This model structure within AGET must firstly account for population equity through demographic weighting before showing full transparent processes for assistance provision.
2. National and local governments employ algorithms to establish Medicaid or Medicare eligibility rules. The models under AGET need to ensure they do not reject people using income metrics when they are inaccurate while providing sufficient explanation and appeal options for their decisions.
3. Algorithms responsible for public school student placements need AGET assessment to prevent the generation of racial and economic divides. Parents along with educators should take part in the model design through participatory approaches.

The governance tools managed by AGET operate to prevent the digital systems from turning into systems of oppression while functioning as paths to inclusive justice access.

Global Implications and Future Directions

There are many nations in the world who respond to the restrictiveness of the software that are used with the help of algorithms. For example, the European Union's AI Act, the U.S. White House Blueprint, and Canada's Directive on Automated Decision-Making, constitute key advancement of the governance system; yet, these frameworks demonstrate scantiness in high-quality equity characteristics.

Since the AGET provides an integrated bundle of practical and theoretical support for governmental integration that enables the amendment of existing systems and software to achieve conformity with individualized requirements and needs, the new governance system should be developed from the time delayed responses that include the public response, and should reform the equity and equitable principles.

Conclusion: Towards an Ethically Programmed Future

Protecting justice through the implementation of algorithmic governance must be considered essential, given the administrative utility of these digital instruments. The societies can ensure the democracy and transparency by integrating the AGET system and their different sectors while keeping in view the importance of fairness. The respective governments should identify how the algorithms are working in their favour or in their society's favour and what are the algorithm that are against the public's interest. The AGET provides and offers comprehensive algorithm that is society friendly and unbiased promoting the fairness among the nation.

Cross-Sector Synergy and Integration

DEFT shows the possible and the most important potential for responding to the social problems by combining its applications in different sectors such as climate change prevention, governance, healthcare, education, and technology. Housing policy creates educational results while environmental conditions determine public health standing and financial choices control policing services together with mental health provision. The interrelated nature between different sectors led to the modular structure of DEFT, which enables the real-time synchronization between multiple equity theories across domains.

The academic goal of this cross-sector synergy exists as a necessity. Any society that wants to handle systemic inequalities with sustainable community-based methods through a comprehensive approach needs this essential development. Government institutions and communities can develop smarter and more responsive just systems through the utilization of interconnected equity models that include EEIT, PEPT, AGET, and EFLT.

FACT: The implementation of smart equity platforms throughout Amsterdam demonstrates how public service delivery improves citizen satisfaction to a level of 45% (SmartCitiesWorld, 2023) thus proving DEFT's concept of sector-agnostic real-time governance based on participatory predictions.

The Power of Interconnected Equity Systems

A municipal area deals with combined issues of environmental threats and education inequality while facing service accessibility inequalities. A DEFT-enabled method unites these separate issues into one unified system instead of working on them independently. A climate adaptation strategy that targets extreme heat events requires special attention in urban areas since these locations affect disadvantaged people who live in substandard housing and lack green public space while facing elevated pollution levels.

The city can employ EEIT to guide tree planting by locating areas with poor tree coverage combined with increased heat island effects through investigating locations, where HDI scores remain low and political capabilities are scarce and communities have traditionally lacked access to urban planning advantages. The plan advances beyond this point.

The city should implement DENT to study successful urban forestry and green infrastructure programs in Medellín (Colombia) and Melbourne (Australia) because these cities use community participation and geo-specific climate data to advance equal green development. Through DENT policymakers gain access to an evolving global practice database that matches local conditions and population characteristics of their specific municipal area.

The EFLT systems establish direct feedback channels that consist of both online applications such as participatory mapping applications and physical forums such as town hall meetings and equity dashboards. Various technological resources permit residents of the community to identify neighbourhood requirements and propose corrective measures while monitoring policy success against resident-driven priorities.

An Integrated Urban Equity Platform

The municipal budget distribution follows an algorithmic procedure (AGET) which uses changeable need indicators consisting of emergency response durations together with income distribution differences and resident-reported infrastructure failures.

Public opinion from resident surveys together with workshops and town hall meetings (EFLT) function as an input system to both affirm and refute algorithmic recommendations using neighbourhood knowledge.

Figure 5.3 illustrates how Algorithmic Governance Equity Theory and Equity Feedback Loop Theory operate together within an integrated urban equity platform linking algorithmic decision making with continuous citizen participation and real time policy adjustment.

This model is not theoretical. Amsterdam together with Seoul and Toronto have established trial versions of such platforms within their cities. The Dutch city of Amsterdam now operates a "Digital Twin" city platform which uses multiple data sets to show how new policies affect its social and economic and environmental conditions in real time according to SmartCitiesWorld (2023). Toronto uses its "Neighbourhood Equity Index" to gather 15 community indicators that show developers where to invest in unequities areas.

The smart city systems of Seoul operate with built-in citizen involvement as a core feature. The "mVoting" application provided by the city lets residents participate in shaping decisions about park and school zoning and it utilizes automated equity monitoring to evaluate how well demographics are included in the outcomes of decision-making processes.

The leading examples confirm that cities need integrated approaches involving multiple sectors to effectively handle twenty-first-century problems.

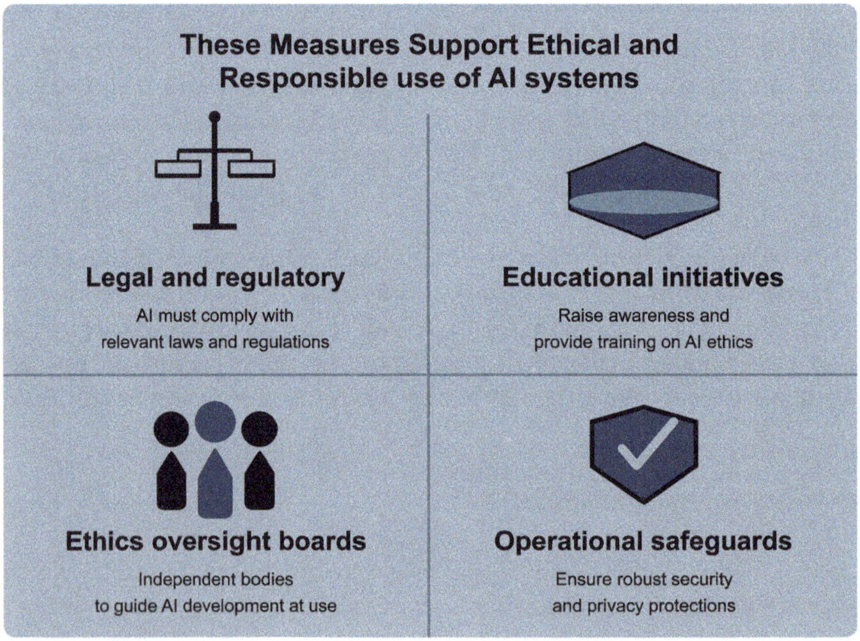

Figure 5.3: Core institutional and operational measures required to ensure ethical and responsible use of artificial intelligence systems.

Dynamic Adaptability Across Systems

DEFT proves itself exceptional because it adapts successfully to new social and environmental and political situations. The framework adapts especially well for urban governance since needs and risks transform swiftly because of population shifts along with changes caused by neighbourhood development and environmental effects and technological changes.

A system built in this manner would behave during a heatwave emergency. Through the equity platform the system could activate emergency cooling centres across locations that EEIT has marked as both heat-prone and insufficiently shaded. The PEPT operational technology would either modify school operating hours or establish remote instruction models for institutions that were projected to experience learning disruptions because of heat-related absenteeism. Real-time emergency budget redirection occurs through AGET after the system receives guidance from transparent explanatory models. Through EFLT service crews would receive instant civil complaints regarding broken public housing air conditioner systems to transport their personnel to the most critical areas.

A system that operates at multiple levels enables public institutions to achieve operational efficiency as well as social fair-mindedness and empathy.

Towards a Systemic Equity Ecosystem

The DEFT approach requires more than technical alignment because it manifests as a fundamental governance change in direction and ethical values. The movement signals a shift from isolated problem reaction systems to active transformation of complete systems. The framework acknowledges the national knowledge and information as the artificial intelligence does and explains that equity is not to separate from the governance principle that is developed with the passage of time.

The various public sectors can enhance the system of an equity by integrating the different systems like predictive PEPT with environmental justice EEIT and AGET and community-friendly EFLT. These systems combine the data, design and mingle into a single operation to the make the more efficient systems that also keep fairness for the upcoming time.

Conclusion

The DEFT provides operational platform that is effective and efficient in enhancing the equity across various departments because it is practical and implementable in the real world. The DEFT offers organized and well-structured plans that make the organizations efficient and effective into the functional activities all over the different sectors is healthcare, education, and environment. The DEFT promotes both to recognize the inequities along with the practical instruments that are fundamental in fighting the justice problems in today's world. The sectors like healthcare and other social systems may get advantages from the theories provided by DEFT like AGET, PEPT, EEIT, HVET, and EFLT. This is the most important ability of the system to be flexible and give important solutions to the ever-growing problems in this society that many face today due to technology and climate changes. Fundamental change emerges in the roles of policymakers together with technologists and educators and healthcare providers along with community members through this approach. Through data support and community participation and feedback transparency equity becomes an initiative which all stakeholders share collectively. This approach establishes an equal standing for decision-making processes making policy recipients into real collaborators who participate in its creation.

This book proceeds to reveal the specific institutional systems and financial approaches as well as organizational dynamics which will establish DEFT within our existing operational structures. Public and private sectors use specific implementation guidelines as well as budgeting frameworks based on equity and long-term system sustainability models and accountability measures.

The objective remains clear which is to construct justice through intentional and collaborative action performed continuously. DEFT exists as the foundation that develops this transformation.

Chapter 6
Ethical Considerations and Challenges

Introduction: The Ethical Imperative of Equity by Design

The use of automatic systems around the globe poses some ethical concerns. The ethical considerations need to be considered for the management because the ethical issues basically make the dynamic equity framework theory (DEFT) limited. DEFT introduces a modern way of attaining equity through its design that incorporates economic and environmental alongside social and emotional elements within an adaptable all-encompassing system. The implications of DEFT become complicated whenever they are applied in the estimation measures and the excessive use in AI; for it raises necessary ethical concerns. Who is behind developing these frameworks? Who deals with these setups? Who is responsible for the codes generated in the computers? The answers to these questions are required by the applications of DEFT.

The uses of this remarkable achievement are very important. It helps the policymakers to make decisions to resolve the problems of the people, who are being treated in some other way, in the society in the health, education, climate, and technology sectors. There is a problem that evolves with these systems. In this regard, the frameworks mainly make decisions by taking control over these crucial steps. The ethical and moral concerns arise when this all is controlled by AI. The frameworks based on AI pose some serious ethical concerns as they have the capability of formulating equitable results besides functional abilities. An organization's unresolved equity issues can endanger the core principle of DEFT regarding equity creation. The DEFT framework uses fair result production to protect technological ethical standards that prevent new systems from producing unfair conditions.

The ethical concerns are evaluated in this chapter before DEFT demonstrates the operational mechanisms that prevent risks from causing harmful impacts on justice. The core characteristics of DEFT is that it establishes a well-mannered framework for the companies to find out the solutions for the ethical dilemmas because it embodies the moral aspects it its algorithm. The systems handled by DEFT gains the moral instructions of providing balanced chances, maintaining equity.

Algorithmic Bias: Designing for Fairness

It is the key moral problems that the system faces before going for its intended purpose. The different systems make different biases. It is to mention that the algorithm has usually biasness towards many decisions.

The systems show discriminations based on colour, race, gender, and religion in the cases of security, crimes, and hiring purposes. The data demonstrates that the

https://doi.org/10.1515/9783112222140-006

women and the economically poor are normally prejudiced and the algorithm shows biasness towards them.

The defined framework of DEFT designs the particular ways that reduce the chances of the systemic biasness towards the groups based on colour, race, gender, and religion especially in the cases of security, crimes, and recruitment objectives. The framework contains a wide range of diverse data so that it produces generalised outcomes to avoid any form of bias. Additionally, DEFT introduces the assessment of various AI systems to avoid any discrimination and biasness. This is how DEFT encounters ethical dilemma as well as biasness, while ensuring fairness, equity, justice, and transparency in all walks of life.

Transparency and Accountability: Building Trust in AI Systems

Creating an environment of trust and belief in the AI systems is necessary. The volatile business landscape makes it imperative to develop a new equity paradigm, which has become necessary rather than a suggestion. This system never simply redistributes assets periodically; instead it automatically and intelligently reacts to actual world circumstances. The novel equity system is possible through the DEFT. The framework should address and utilize the existing changes in technology along with structures of data so that the fairness standards can be established for the upcoming era.

The design and deployment of AI systems need to be transparent according to DEFT to resolve the existing concerns. DEFT requires every algorithm with public access to all code components whether they are open source or available for independent audit by expert public observers. The complete view into AI system functioning allows both public values to align with system operations and enables outcome responsibility mechanisms.

DEFT requires developers along with operators of AI systems to establish accountable systems through which they take responsibility for decisions executed by their AI implementations. DEFT achieves its primary goal through ongoing algorithm audits which use separate demographics to detect how AI systems affect different population segments thus blocking structural inequality reinforcement. Organizations must deliver understandable explanations to people who experience algorithmic outcomes to ensure complex algorithms do not protect unethical choices.

FACT: According to a 2022 EU survey results indicated that 72% of citizens did not comprehend how AI made its decisions which proves why DEFT needs both public algorithmic transparency together with participatory oversight.

Privacy and Security: Protecting Sensitive Data

AI systems that need real-time data for decisions have made protection of privacy together with data security into critical concerns. The analysis of sensitive personal information about health records education and finances enables prediction of outcomes to distribute resources. However, the collection, storage, and analysis of this data raise significant privacy risks. The present status of digital surveillance poses actual threats to the illicit usage of personal information that can reveal data outside accepted user terms.

DEFT implements risk management for privacy which enables security measures to protect privacy while processing knowledge-based data. DEFT implements a full-scale data protection system that safeguards individual personal information when preserving its intended purpose. Building privacy-protecting systems with control-based data management systems and secure decentralized frameworks allows organizations to develop systems through DEFT.

The personal data collection methods in DEFT include absolute data transparency combined with mandatory individual consent. The public requires full knowledge about data practices although they should understand from whom their data reaches and when it will remain stored. Informed consent stands as a fundamental method for data user systems to establish trust with the public because it protects the ethical and self-determined nature of data collection operations.

Conclusion: A Framework for Ethical AI in Public Life

The merits of technology and other related stuff have though positives; yet, they possess serious moral dilemma. Systems that employ these technologies require ethical principles to be implemented during design phase alongside operational phase because their governance role is expected to grow. However, the ethical security and privacy is ensured while using DEFT as it guards the users from being ethically manipulated through its vigorous defensive techniques.

To ensure ethical practices, the DEFT framework also encourages the different businesses to implement the equitable and ethical procedures into their algorithm and possible decision-making processes such as recruitment policies and the product development stages along with corporate social responsibility activities. DEFT enhances the businesses by offering them the pathway to go beyond the basic outcomes of the CSR activities and making the profits along with social welfare.

Algorithmic Bias: Detecting and Preventing Inequitable Outcomes

The algorithms in many systems show discriminations and biasness towards certain groups in the society. This further weakens the ability of the system. It forms so many biased forums and makes decisions that are favourable for some and unfavourable for many which is enhancing inequity in the social order. This further develops negative thoughts and comments about certain groups that are already facing these prejudices from the elite groups in the society. There are many societal differences in our society on the basis of gender, colour, race, and nationality such as Black and White tussle. The systems fail when their algorithms contain unnecessary biasness while making necessary decisions.

The systems containing the bias are developed by the scientists and the developers because they do errors while compiling the codes. The unnecessary and unwanted biases create problems for the people in the society. It imposes negative impacts on individuals. The DEFT framework does work in other way. It includes the ways of converting the biased systems into fair and just ones. This makes DEFT stand tall and unique.

The Roots of Algorithmic Bias

Previous data serves as a critical foundation for algorithmic operations because this data allows them to discover patterns and make their decisions. The training process of algorithms with social biases within their input data enables these biases to manifest when the algorithms conduct operations.

The teaching data that enters the hiring algorithm originates from historical employment records which trains it to pick male candidates prior to female candidates when men consistently outnumber women in the workforce. The predictive policing algorithm obtains training data from police reports that may inherently contain law enforcement discrimination which makes it focus on specific neighbourhoods resulting in biased outcomes.

A third source of bias emerges when developers choose how to build algorithms and what presumptions they include in the development process. Implementation teams responsible for system development need to determine several essential processes related to variable selection while weighing procedures and establishing performance metrics. The system will naturally incorporate bias through two factors: incomplete human diversity knowledge and unrecognized designer prejudices. The situation becomes more severe when technical teams do not include representatives from non-dominant communities since discrimination occurs throughout the development cycle.

Autonomous system operations generate bias permanence through the independent decision-making capabilities of the system. The process of predictive policing algorithm-generated law enforcement targeting in particular areas produces data showing higher crime numbers within those geographic regions.

Case Studies of Algorithmic Bias

Surveillance systems are used for security strive to detect white faces more successfully than they identify faces of both Asian and Black people within the demographic. Surveillance and law enforcement practices become unbalanced because flawed technological systems force people especially from marginalized communities to face unjustifiable observation. The misidentification capabilities of facial recognition in police work remains concerning because they can result in incorrect arrests that violate civil rights and freedoms.

Research at MIT Media Lab published by Buolamwini and Gebru (2018) showed commercial facial recognition programs failed to recognize dark-skinned faces and female faces better than they recognized light-skinned male faces. The systems displayed multiple types of discrimination which produced severe problems in surveillance functions and public security systems. Facial recognition technology deployed at airports operates for identity confirmation but temporary or permanent confiscation of individuals arises when the system produces wrong matches.

The domain of predictive policing demonstrates that algorithm systems historically focused their surveillance on racial populations found predominantly in low-income areas. The SyRI (System Risk Indication) scandal stands out as a significant case because it happened in the Netherlands. The judicial system ruled the Dutch government's utilization of the SyRI system as discriminatory during 2020. Officials employed the system for welfare fraud detection which resulted in heightened risks being found predominantly within low-income areas with high minority populations.

The algorithm applied socioeconomic criteria including employment records and income together with other factors to detect fraudsters; yet its opacity and data prejudice led to thousands of incorrect welfare program rejections and deportations (Human Rights Watch, 2020). Genuine systems that operate without oversight generate adverse effects against defenceless groups within vulnerable populations.

The DEFT also helps the researchers who conduct various research activities of different but unique fields to minimize the biasness and inequality.

Inclusion of Diverse Datasets

The use of various experiences and identities in datasets serves developers to build systems that are accurate and fair. During face recognition system development, teams must authoritatively include pictures from all racial backgrounds together with ethnic groups and different genders. The inclusion of diverse datasets reduces the possibility that the system will show inadequate performance for particular groups just like reported by the studies by the AI Now Institute and MIT Media Lab.

Intersectional Impact Assessments

The execution of DEFT depends significantly on carrying out intersectional impact assessments. The evaluations assess when disparate elements including racial background and gender together with social status and disability status produce particular system experiences for individuals. Black women experience the world differently from both their racial identity and gender identity because race and gender relations create unique interaction effects between them. DEFT performs intersectional impact assessments that help understand all effects that algorithmic systems have on specific vulnerable communities so these potential impacts can receive proper attention.

Participatory Design with Affected Communities

DEFT supports a practice of ensuring community-based participation during the design and regulatory stages of algorithmic systems affecting those communities most significantly. The participatory design process grants representation to people vulnerable to discriminatory results especially the groups of low-income earners and minority races and marginalized genders. The involvement of affected communities helps developers build systems that address important needs and concerns of their specific communities particularly those likely to be affected.

There are plenty of nations that are getting it into practice the welfare and improving the social health by collaborating the moral values and long-term merits. The fast-paced increasing climate problems and disunity among various groups on the earth along with psychological disorders encourage the concerned to create straight relation among the financial, human, and environmental objectives.

Conclusion: A Framework for Fairer AI

Fairness in equity is one of the most pressing issues that the systems face and public trust is lost in frameworks. Using primary data, this study examines the economic, social, cultural, and legal factors of biasness. The research investigates how income levels, employment status, education, social norms, cultural values, and perceptions of the system influence the behaviour towards bias. The DEFT aims to offer valuable insights for the concerned authorities and policymakers to develop better strategies to reduce biasness, enhance public confidence in the system, and hence improve the overall system.

Transparency and Accountability: Building Public Trust

The implementation of DEFT proves to be strong social infrastructure components that deliver additional environmental advantages and results in creating friendly relations and trust among the public. The initiative accomplishes urban restructuring which gives higher priority to people instead of vehicles while simultaneously creating communal bonds between residents. The local community members feel safer because the area has encouraged stronger connections with neighbours and residents actively participate in community-based events. The initiative enables architectural constructs by welcoming citizens to actively engage with civic initiatives.

The Public Algorithmic Transparency Framework (PATF)

DEFT provides the Public Algorithmic Transparency Framework (PATF) as its structured system that enables public understanding of decision-making algorithms accessible to citizens through transparent processes. Through the PATF systems avoid presenting as unexamined boxes because they welcome public evaluation together with meaningful review and participation from the public. It includes three key components:

Public Documentation of Algorithmic Logic

All public-sector algorithms in PATF require documentation that must demonstrate clear accessible information to stakeholders. The documentation must provide detailed information about its intended purpose as well as its assigned variables and their weights and also describe how outputs are calculated. DEFT stresses that algorithms need plain-language visual explanations that enable ordinary people and specifically those who are affected to grasp the system functions. People who understand how decision-making processes operate have the capability to check institutions for proper accountability.

Open-Source Access or Third-Party Review Panels

Through DEFT the authors advocate for two alternatives to boost expert scrutiny and accountability which include algorithm open-source exposure or the creation of independent third-party review boards. Technology experts alongside academic researchers and watchdog groups gain full access to open-source code because this enables them to find bugs and establish methods to strengthen it. The DEFT organization supports the implementation of trusted review panels consisting of experts from different fields together with civil society advocates and community representatives who would review systems that cannot share their code in an open-source fashion. The panels would receive authority to execute periodic ratings as well as investigate equity consequences before issuing public assessment documents about their outcomes.

Clear Communication of Data Use

Organizations need to maintain clear disclosure which details their data sources as well as their data usage under transparency requirements. Public sector algorithm systems need to show mandatory information about their data management activities and decision-making processes while providing explanations related to data collection and storage. The public needs detailed understanding of which population characteristics are processed in combination with health records and neighbourhood information by crisis patient selection algorithms to determine sequence positioning. Users gain better system understanding which allows them to test the validity of data inputs while monitoring their appropriate use.

The equity feedback loop theory (EFLT) acts as a key operational tool that enables the integration of equity feedback.

Obtaining visibility through transparency enables the implementation of essential accountability systems. DEFT advances its goal by installing intentional public oversight, which integrates directly into operational frameworks of algorithmic systems. The EFLT core segment of DEFT creates an EFLT for continuous feedback-based correction of equity irregularities.

Through EFLT community members receive a parallel capability to identify adverse effects between their active participation and the official reporting framework. DEFT implements feedback systems that enable communities to document various disparities between public funding and low-income school resources and housing assistance frameworks that affect big families. Three primary processes in the system enable equity recalibration: auditing systems, technical algorithm changes and complete policy investigations.

As a part of EFLT feedback processes receive validation systems to ensure they avoid restricted symbolic communication channels. The system operates continuous monitoring for community members to inspect and assist in developing their equity structures. Through its approach the system provides clear visibility and power sharing that enables marginalized groups to influence the governing technology systems which affect them.

Democratic Alignment and Civic Trust

The structured algorithmic governance achieves democratic alignment by combining PATF and EFLT into necessary elements to operate with DEFT. The public attains transparent information when individuals accept responsibility to fulfil accountability tasks. The people are governed by the democracy that is digital and modern. These practices are normal nowadays in many nations. They have built-in quality systems. The DEFT framework is appropriate for this. It discloses the systems before applying it for enhancement of justice, equity, and transparency.

Conclusion: Trust as Infrastructure

The systems require the due trust and belief in them. Policy recognition of different cultures functions as an essential key to achieve trust. Administrative policies that appreciate and honour trust in systems within a community space create stronger feelings of belongingness among its members. Inclusive societies form through providing language services and indigenous governing framework backing together with multicultural art installations that enable community members to see reflections of themselves with respect. Public policy demonstrates either advisement between citizens through deficient design or creation of political solidarity through its implementation. However, the ethical safeguard system, as illustrated in Figure 6.1, will ensure public policy generates solidarity.

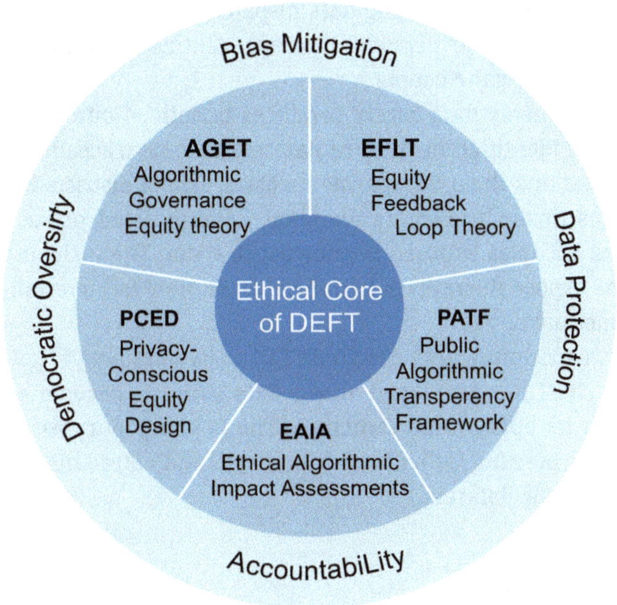

Figure 6.1: Ethical safeguard system.

Privacy and Security: Balancing Data Utilization and Individual Rights

Every person retains the fundamental protection of their private security through secure data management that defends against unfair and unlawful exploitation in addition to discrimination practices.

PCED functions as the main operational principle of the DEFT to resolve ethical conflicts between these fundamental rights. The combination of operational principles allows institutions to employ an ethical and comprehensive equity analysis method that helps reduce adverse effects on individuals and safeguards their rights together with their autonomy.

Why Privacy Matters in Equity Frameworks

The currently used systems demand every important point of data for the execution. This is done to find the solutions to the discrepancies in economic as well as housing themes. This solution needs the data in ins and outs. So, this poses severe ethical concerns such as data theft. The third parties collecting data dispatch and share the private data with different companies for their personal interests. All this scenario creates a sense of distrust and doubt among the people.

The positive intention behind using data rarely produces beneficial outcomes. Multiple instances exist where de-identified healthcare datasets become traceable to specific individuals when analysts link them to separate datasets. School districts implementing monitoring systems through learning analytics have violated privacy when student behavioural data becomes exposed beknownst to them. The incidents demonstrate that organizations expose themselves to danger when they fail to establish stringent data protection measures.

The DEFT proposes privacy-conscious equity design (PCED) as its solution.

The PCED framework that DEFT has developed allows data ethics to become an integral part of design through its operational structure. The primary purpose of PCED serves twofold objectives: protecting individuals from harm and extracting the maximum public value from equitable datasets.

Anonymized and Encrypted Data Pipelines

Every entity performing equity assessments must begin with encrypting data while maintaining anonymity as a default security measure. The data anonymization process requires researchers to remove personal identification details consisting of names as well as addresses and ID numbers. The encryption process generates data that stays incomprehensible to unauthorized parties even if they intercept or access the data. The combination of anonymization and encryption layers achieves two protection objectives which makes it extremely challenging for unethical parties to exploit data.

Differential Privacy Techniques

DEFT endorses differential privacy which adds mathematical noise to datasets through statistical methods to stop the identification of persons. Institutions using differential privacy tools perform analyses between groups of people without revealing any specific person's identifiable information to the analysis. Differential privacy techniques successfully protect user privacy through the addition of statistical noise to data which Apple and the U.S. Census Bureau already apply in their analyses.

Data Minimization Protocols

The foundation of PCED includes a requirement to acquire data that meets the essential needs for equity tasks. Establishments too frequently acquire extensive database collections simply for contingency purposes which results in superfluous risk exposure areas. Every data request under PCED requires clear explanations to be approved. The model only requires income bracket information when it satisfies equity conditions because this sufficient data does not need additional salary details. The requirement for full addresses becomes unnecessary after institutions confirm zip code serves their geographic needs. The "less is more" principle decreases contact points that establish faith in operations.

Time-Bound Data Retention

PCED requires organizations to maintain specific regulations regarding the duration that equity data should remain accessible. An uncompromising data deletion routine should be implemented after analysis and intervention where the information moves to secure storage in forms that protect identity.

Developing Moral Values

Due to these reasons DEFT promotes joint work between data scientists along with civil rights advocates cybersecurity experts legal scholars and impacted communities. The coalition partnerships work to establish privacy measures that honour democratic values as opposed to providing ease for companies.

The public needs clear explanations about data collection rules together with descriptions of security systems along with detailed information about how collected data will be used through accessible language. People need to understand all the information about what data gets collected along with reasons for collection as well as its duration and methods of collection. The public must receive data governance charters through DEFT that explain equity-relevant data collection and analysis projects in all their fundamental aspects.

Conclusion: Privacy as a Precondition for Trust

Justice exists as exposure rather than as fairness whenever privacy remains absent. DEFT envisions privacy to serve as a fundamental requirement that grants its equity work full legitimacy. People need to experience security to disclose personal information. The data user base must be assured that their data will be utilized to generate positive advantages instead of negative consequences.

PCED serves as an ethical methodology to merge equity assessment capabilities with fundamental human privacy requirements. The privacy is one of the key preferences of DEFT as it takes it into account from the very first stage of data collection to data running and saving it with full security, making the system effective, efficient, reliable, and trustworthy.

The Ethics of Automation: Who Decides and How?

The equity frameworks must handle the ethical concerns because of the automated systems. There are questions to be answered: Who develops those systems that have great impacts on human lives? Who formulates the policies? Who allows the automated software in decision-making and policymaking for various sectors such as healthcare, economic, technological, and security? At what stage the data theft happens? These are the questions that need to be answered.

The security behaviours are those activities that involve influencing the private data, including the act of disseminating the data, undertaking activities and presenting fake claims in the names of general public. Financial capacity that comes with employment standards and physical earnings greatly influence the ability of a person to involve in this. Hence the financially weaker individuals are found to be more likely to indulge in data theft in cases of higher rates than those of higher income levels accompanied by economic stability as they have more to lose in terms of legal consequences of their actions or the lack of them.

The people behind the DEFT are of the view that the privacy of the people should be the priority of the system. The algorithms that are automated must be well monitored so that no incident of the data theft and moral dismay occur. For all, the objective of justice and fairness should not be forgotten.

Ethical Review Boards for Algorithmic Systems

DEFT purposes the typical boards for the monitoring of the automated systems to ensure privacy security for the public. This can be done with the help of "Ethical Review Boards (ERBs)" which would essentially assess the systems that they are not breaching any ethical principles rather they are perfect morally. These would have sets of experts of the field that will ensure transparency and fairness.

There must be criteria that the relevant algorithms must go through to be able for further conduct. Apart from it, the timely assessments should be carried out to see the ongoing performances. Such initiatives would surely enhance the public trust and confidence in the systems.

Ethical Algorithm Impact Assessments (EAIA)

"Ethical Algorithm Impact Assessments (EAIA)" is developed by DEFT as provisional assessment metrics for conducting ethical and moral evaluations. It happens before the system is implemented. The core areas are:

1. Discrimination on the basis of gender, race, colour, and creed.
2. The goals are aligned with public interests.
3. The public should be given information about how the algorithms work.

These evaluations tend to work as instruments to analyse any moral or ethical differences. The relevant people might go through the policies and the concerned documents.

Conclusion

Conclusion: Responsibility in the Age of Automation

The development of policies for equity-based issues creates increased human responsibility instead of eliminating the need for human responsibilities. The essential nature of the circumstance together with past technological struggles creates a necessity for humans to maintain full control of fairness decisions. The ethical automation aspects of DEFT establish specific domains to define machine capability boundaries as well as proper frameworks for machine operation control.

DEFT offers an assessment system that keeps reviewing the software and tracks down any discrepancy in the system. The framework is automated and hence proving the best use of self-evaluation.

Conclusion: Ethics as a Structural Component of DEFT

Active involvement of community members along with policymakers should be central during the process of creating and executing the ethical policies. Community involvement within policy decisions enables moral measures to match the requirements and essential needs of people who face the discrimination and biasness everyday. People who take part in such collaborative efforts establish better trust levels and raise accountability while producing enduring solutions.

The framework of DEFT requires ethics to be as essential component. Moral justice requires two main strategies – combining ethical policies with justice principles and involving local communities in choosing development and moral decisions. Additionally, disadvantaged regions should receive investments for green systems to make them feel owned and cared.

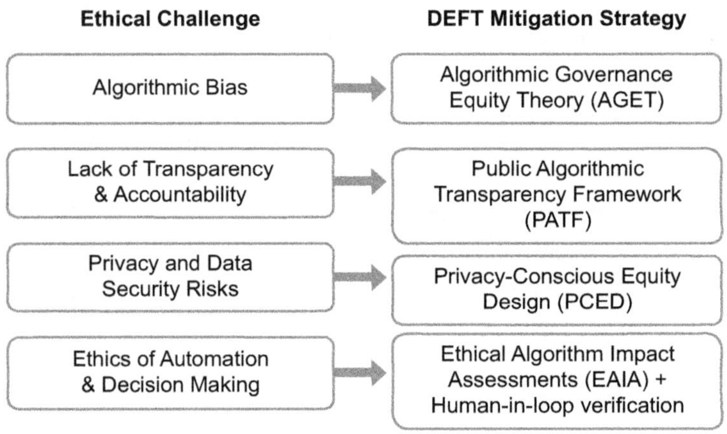

Figure 6.2: Reducing ethical dilemma.

Equity achieves true adaptability when its definition incorporates both equality and ethical contents. Figure 6.2 shows the summary of the strategies with which DEFT mitigates the listed ethical challenges. The material exchange of money cannot be the sole interpretation of equity. The basic elements of ethics and mores alongside income and employment deliver substantial value to equity but these essential components fail to explain the complete justice framework of society. Elements establish human survival capacities in individual lives and community organizational systems that drive long-term social standards across multiple generations. Ethics is therefore core outcome of DEFT.

The Ethical Scaffolding of DEFT

The systems require the due trust and belief in them. Policy recognition of different cultures functions as an essential key to achieve trust. Administrative policies that appreciate and honour trust in systems within a community space create stronger feelings of belongingness among its members. Inclusive societies form through providing language services and Indigenous governing framework backing together with multicultural art installations that enable community members to see reflections of themselves with respect. Public policy demonstrates either advisement between citizens through deficient design or creation of political solidarity through its implementation. As a part of EFLT feedback processes receive validation systems to ensure they avoid restricted symbolic communication channels. The system operates continuous monitoring for community members to inspect and assist in developing their equity structures. Through its approach the system provides clear visibility and power sharing that enables marginalized groups to influence the governing technology systems which affect them.

From Policy Aspiration to Operational Reality

The foundation of institutions designed for ethical decision-making becomes possible when combined with programs for moral training delivered to equity developers coupled with ethical software development systems before creating legal frameworks to track algorithms and establishing multijurisdictional organizations that protect digital rights.

Through DEFT the authors advocate for two alternatives to boost expert scrutiny and aspiration which include algorithm operational exposure or the creation of independent third-party review boards. Technology experts alongside academic researchers and watchdog groups gain full access to open-source code because this enables them to find bugs and establish methods to strengthen it. The DEFT organization supports the implementation of trusted review panels consisting of experts from different fields together with civil society advocates and community representatives who would review systems that cannot share their code in an open-source fashion. The panels would receive authority to execute periodic ratings as well as investigate equity consequences before issuing public assessment documents about their outcomes.

DEFT bases its foundation on ethical standards that produce innovative and efficient systems in addition to creating durable humane and fair products. The achievement of better systems represents just one piece of our objectives which include the development of a future we envision being more desirable.

Chapter 7
DEFT and Global Governance

In this chapter, we would see how the different governing bodies utilize the dynamic equity framework theory (DEFT) to combat the systematic inequalities. Owing to increased globalization, several threatening problems have taken place. Policymaking through traditional global governance depends on outdated indicator systems along with hierarchical approaches and set policy periods that are unable to adapt to modern global crisis evolution.

The DEFT system implements a set of dynamic principles and sub-theories including real-time redistribution and algorithmic equity governance and participatory feedback loops and privacy-conscious data structures to help international institutions and states and multinational corporations build data-informed and justice-oriented systems. The systems feature the ability to provide customized solutions matching indigenous requirements as a part of their universal collaborative framework.

This chapter examines how DEFT should be implemented into operational structures of organizations including United Nations and World Bank and World Health Organization and transnational alliances. The research evaluates DEFT implementation by private-sector global development actors dealing with technology and finance to enhance accountability systems with inclusive results. As a solution we must exceed useless statements about equity by implementing operational plans that establish justice as an active transformative practice in global administrative bodies.

Introduction: The Global Equity Deficit

The global governance system reveals an ironic dilemma during the twenty-first century because major international institutions including the United Nations (UN) and World Bank and International Monetary Fund (IMF) and World Health Organization (WHO) among others that were founded for global cooperation bring about worsening inequalities between and within different parts of the world. There is a huge growing gap between the rich and the poor. This gap is widening as the income inequalities are persistent around the globe.

The major frameworks used in policymaking are out-dated as they contain differences among the social classes. The policies made with the help of these algorithms favour the upper class or elites but ignore the struggling unit in the society. Those who are in power are mainly supported by these discriminatory systems. Whereas the lower or disadvantaged groups become prey to the biased treatments of the system. At the governance side, the people in charge are supported by the systems. In this way, the inequality prevails in the society with many economic gaps. This is the

https://doi.org/10.1515/9783112222140-007

inability of government as well as the used systems in decision-making and policy-making.

The countries across the globe are provided with the same amount of funds for the climate change. This is unfair in toto. The underdeveloped countries are the most victims of the inhumane activities of the developed nations that cause pollutions in the underprivileged areas of the world. The world must understand that this is not the way to eradicate the climate dilemma in all its forms. The developed nations do not need that much attention as the developing do. These unfair policymaking of the governments is condemned in the perspective of DEFT.

The DEFT provides the framework that is very helpful and implementable to all the world, eliminating injustice in all its forms. The victimized nations should be given more preferences while a little should be paid to the countries causing unnecessary environments degradation through industrialization and overproduction.

DEFT principles should direct international financial institutions to develop new development funding methods that consider past discriminatory treatment combined with future resilience capabilities in place of standard GDP evaluation systems. DEFT presents a distinctive set of advantages for governing climate change at a global scale. Climate finance structures currently receive complaints for their unclear processes and donor-control system that provides benefits to nations with strong proposal writing skills and middle-income status. By adopting a DEFT-aligned method organizations would establish adaptable funding redistribution systems that use current climate vulnerability measurements along with community input to shape their decision-making processes. A system that implements these measures will elevate the validity of international climate finance as it increases benefits for frontline communities.

A mind and methodological change must occur to integrate DEFT concepts into global governance systems. Institutions need to implement equity by developing a process that is continuously evolving through a technologically enabled collaborative system with inclusivity at its heart. This transformation necessitates collaboration between technologists, policymakers, data scientists, ethicists, and local communities. The change requires new accountability systems to distribute authority to diverse communities and enable stakeholders who experience global choices to influence the development and assessment of these choices.

DEFT by itself does not act as a complete solution for solving problems. Its successful deployment requires strong institutional dedication together with appropriate infrastructure support and moral undertaking from all stakeholders. The current decline of multilateralism and rising climate pressures and inequality make it impossible to keep implementing previous methods. The world requires governance models to match the dynamic characteristics and interconnected framework and equity principles of its current challenges (Figure 7.1).

This chapter demonstrates the process of integrating DEFT within global institutions while concluding multilateral collaborations and propagating it across international borders. The adoption of DEFT allows global governance to achieve its historical purpose through order maintenance and the construction of an equitable justice system worldwide.

FACT: The World Inequality Report (2022) indicates that global wealth distribution shows top 10% control 76% of total assets and bottom 50% holds only 2% through this unequal distribution causing global systems to become unstable and decreasing worldwide trust levels.

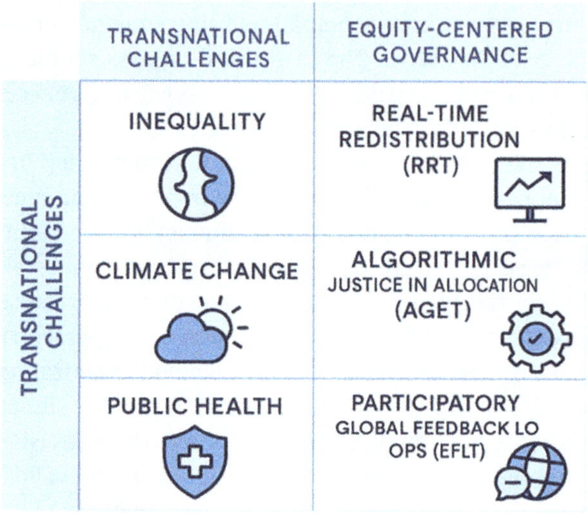

Figure 7.1: Global governance DEF.

Global Policy Applications: DEFT at the Multilateral Level

Traditional international governance models together with traditional systems for distributing aid have proven insufficient to accurately handle the complex needs of inequality during times of rising global unpredictability. The DEFT presents institutions at the international level with an innovative solution through policies that remain adaptable while respecting ethical principles and showing proactive responses. The application of DEFT will be studied through the framework of the United Nations (UN) and World Bank institutions at the global governance level.

The United Nations and Adaptive Equity

FACT: DEFT serves as a necessary dynamic tool because UN SDG progress reports indicate that 800 million people continue in extreme poverty while low-income nations have revealed significant slowness in education recovery after COVID (UN SDG Report 2023).

The United Nations functions as the leading global association to support international cooperation as well as defend human rights and enable sustainable development. The Universal Declaration of Human Rights along with the Sustainable Development Goals (SDGs) enables the UN to create standards that direct fair development between nations. These concepts remain incomplete when implemented since existing data gaps and organizational inflexibility create a delay in meeting new circumstances.

The SDGs have spent nine years as active guidelines; yet multiple goals regarding health equity (SDG 3), quality education (SDG 4), and climate action (SDG 13) appear difficult to achieve. The major cause of this shortfall exists in the policy-design deficits that do not align with evolving target-population realities. The identified equity deficits are illustrated in Figure 7.2. The toolkit for equity provided by DEFT responds to such gaps through context-driven development.

1. Algorithmic Governance Equity Theory (AGET) in Humanitarian Logistics

The UNHCR alongside the WFP along with other humanitarian agencies apply artificial intelligence technologies and predictive analysis for generating resources and distribution planning during refugee emergencies. The systems run the risk of maintaining years-long biases because they lack proper equity framework implementation. AGET enables responsible implementation and monitoring of systems integrating AI with logistics to achieve proper individual vulnerability-based decision-making rather than static allocation methods.

Within a refugee camp all displaced persons receive equal representation yet women-led families and disabled persons encounter intensely higher levels of adversity. The AGET system requires detailed data collection and automated audit processes because this ensures humanitarian efforts remain fair and accurate.

2. Equity Feedback Loop Theory (EFLT) in Participatory Aid Design

Interventions that start from the top level frequently fail to grasp how the genuine experiences look for the people they seek to help. The EFLT system fights this problem through the implementation of community feedback protocols that work directly with program creation and delivery procedures. Real-time community feedback about aid interventions can come from mobile surveys that are supported by local council participation and regional focus group meetings.

A United Nations-supported educational project faces the challenge of reaching rural female students because local cultural practices act as barriers to their enrolment. Such gaps in the implementation of EFLT can be identified through community feedback processes that would enable prompt intervention by rethinking the aid approach through mobile learning applications or gender-responsive curriculum development. People who need equity to be directed at them get to help guide its development process.

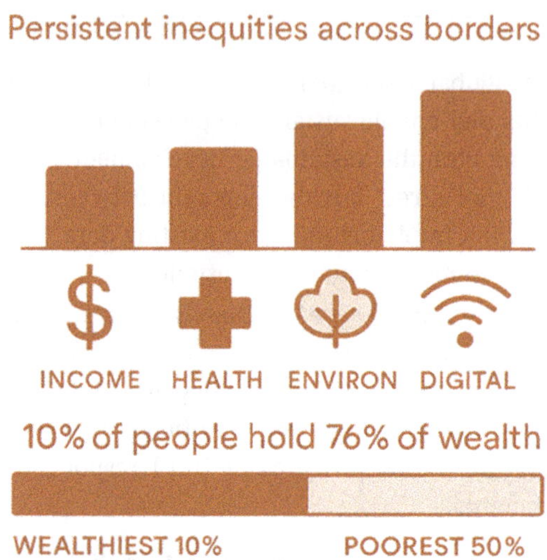

Figure 7.2: Equity deficit.

3. Temporal Equity Shift Theory (TEST) for Reparative Justice
TEST creates an additional time frame within equity systems that puts historical perspectives at the centre of resource management. Structural adjustment policies and colonial exploitation mechanisms together with geopolitical marginalization continue to influence many countries' progress towards development. TEST enables the UN to establish reparative justice within its programming when it directs assistance towards countries with past disadvantages.

Climate resilience funding from the Green Climate Fund (GCF) can be distributed through an application of TEST principles. TEST uses current climate exposure and historical emission disparities to determine how grants are distributed to developing nations instead of using standard grant allocation methods. The methodology grants first priority status to countries that have the smallest role in global warming generation but bear the highest consequences.

The World Bank and Dynamic Equity Lending

Through its financial assistance and expert advice and technical support against economic development the World Bank develops the framework for economic growth. GDP per capita measurement alongside fiscal performance indicators fail to capture the complexity of equity despite being applied by the World Bank as main assessment tools.

DEFT's Holistic Value Equity Theory (HVET) provides Bank personnel with a new system for analysing loan eligibility along with designing lending terms and establishing performance standards.

FACT: The World Bank's Global Economic Prospects (2023) declared that income equality between wealthy and poor countries experienced its first period of stasis in numerous decades thus demonstrating the minimal worth of fixed GDP-based financing methods.

---

1. Expanding Evaluation Metrics with HVET

GDP functions as an inappropriate sole metric to measure a country's overall development potential as well as its citizens' quality of life. HVET presents an assessment framework combining multiple elements which consist of:

1. Human Development Index (HDI) components like health and education
2. Climate Risk Indices
3. Inequality-Adjusted Social Resilience Scores
4. Gender Equity Indices
5. Informal Labor Market Metrics

Two countries that have equal GDPs might demonstrate enormous differences regarding their gender equality and their exposure to climate changes. With HVET the World Bank would offer loans to vulnerable countries after reflecting their distinctive conditions through adapted terms.

2. Dynamic Equity Lending Structures

The World Bank should move towards a Dynamic Equity Lending (DEL) system according to assessment results from HVET. Loan requirements would become adaptive under this model since borrower conditions would measure through real-time data monitoring and public governance participation.

The main components of DEL consist of:

1. The lending interest rate system offers lower payments to countries that achieve improvements in social equity metrics.
2. Time-based disbursements: accelerated funding in response to crises such as natural disasters or pandemics.
3. Borrowers would receive partial debt cancellation through forgiveness clauses when the borrowed funds successfully create equity gaps.
4. Nationwide governance benefits from this method because it promotes fairness and rewards ethical governance practices at a national level.

3. Inclusive Technical Assistance

The World Bank uses its position to formulate the strategies that guide national development alongside funding financial support. DEFT should lead technical assistance programs to redesign their education activities which focus on developing public administrator skills in equity literacy to enable fair policy execution.

Borrowing nations should implement workshops along with equity simulation labs and digital equity dashboards which will establish DEFT as a governance tool and mind-set in global economic governance. Including DEFT within operational frameworks of organizations such as the UN and World Bank will boost the worldwide governance of equity. DEFT implements concrete operational methods from historical understanding and data-based decision-making to support development finance and humanitarian aid distribution. The implementation of DEFT enables global equity closures while bolstering international cooperation strength in light of world fragmentation.

Comprehensive Case Study: Global Pandemic Response and the Need for DEFT

Background: COVID-19 and the Equity Crisis

COVID-19 caused more than health problems in the world because it created a crisis that exposed harsh divisions between different communities. The pandemic unveiled existing inequalities that existed between global health systems coupled with vulnerabilities in worldwide political organizations and social class stability. The coronavirus virus caused no distinctions between people but the worldwide reaction to it established clear divisions among different groups. The extreme inequalities between countries became visible as well as the inequalities within communities through inadequate vaccine supply and funding as well as restricted resource accessibility. By the end of 2020 high-income countries with 16% of the total global population had acquired more than 70% of early vaccine doses per data from Duke Global Health Innovation Center (2021). The Global South had to fight for access to fundamental supplies such as PPE and ventilators during this time while other nations secured these basic materials.

The COVAX initiative which functioned as a partnership between nations to distribute vaccines equally failed in reaching its purpose. COVAX fell short in its mission because it received insufficient funding as well as faced barriers from countries conserving vaccines and lacking regulatory authority to enforce equitable vaccine distribution. According to data from the World Health Organization up to 2021 ended with more than 90% of population from low-income nations remaining unvaccinated. The unfair distribution of vaccines went beyond simple logistic and bureaucratic malfunction.

FACT: The 16% of the world's population that constitutes high-income countries received 70% of initial COVID-19 vaccines through 2021 until 90% of people in low-income countries remained without any vaccine doses (Duke Global Health Innovation Center, WHO, 2021).

Lack of adaptive ethical and equity-centred design principles in the existing governance model led to the outcome.

Structural Failures and the Need for a New Framework

The problems witnessed during the COVID-19 era ran deeper than operational difficulties because they stemmed from structural defects. Such an international arrangement put national strength and diplomatic connections and ancient power structures ahead of present-day requirements and defenceless states. Time-fixed vaccine distribution and static aid distribution mechanisms combined with inadequate community input caused preventable mortality in addition to sustained lockdowns and economic breakdowns in the world's disadvantaged areas. The response lacked a flexible global governance structure which could apply ethical standards at large scale and practically make equity implementation possible. The global pandemic response would have been transformed through implementation of the DEFT.

The application of DEFT dynamic framework theory would have generated a global pandemic equity management system

1. Real-Time Redistribution Theory (RRT)

RRT as part of DEFT could establish a worldwide dashboard that combined dynamic data for infections and hospitals along with population density statistics and healthcare capabilities and vaccination systems maintenance. This interactive system utilized real-time calculating algorithms to distribute medical materials and vaccines while pandemic conditions changed. The RRT model from DEFT would enable continuous adjustments of quotas through updated data.

This solution would prove most advantageous for countries including India and Brazil due to their extensive infection outbreaks and limited vaccine access alongside overwhelmed healthcare operations. The system would have allowed for accelerated global responses directed towards places with the highest needs instead of following political considerations.

2. Algorithmic Governance Equity Theory (AGET)

The previous distribution systems based their strategies on basic indicators including country population numbers and Gross Domestic Product. The framework of DEFT incorporates AGET as its essential component that supports the integration of multiple extensive variables into algorithmic distribution systems including age composition data alongside chronic disease rates together with density statistics and frontline worker exposure analysis and historical inequality measurement.

With the implementation of AGET during the COVID-19 pandemic healthcare authorities would have focused vaccine delivery strategies on vulnerable subnational areas. Under regular audit review systems the algorithms would stay open for public transparency through third-party oversight or open-source performance verification to prevent systematic disadvantage of any region.

3. Equity Feedback Loop Theory (EFLT)

Community feedback proved essential in identifying the biggest shortcoming of worldwide pandemic management which failed to seek input from the local population. Most top-level intervention strategies failed to incorporate local knowledge and cultural considerations together with up-to-date access barriers. The EFLT component of DEFT creates participatory feedback paths which let healthcare personnel alongside civil society groups and private citizens collaborate during both pandemic strategy development and assessment stages.

EFLT would have provided Sub-Saharan African communities with a reporting system to track mRNA vaccine cold chain storage problems which would enable global health agencies to distribute more stable vaccine options. NGOs observing local misinformation trends in Southeast Asia could speed up their information sharing so education campaigns could start immediately in affected areas.

4. Privacy-Conscious Equity Design (PCED)

The pursuit of equity analytics through mathematical models should never compromise the privacy boundaries of nations nor their territorial independence. DEFT implements PCED as a procedure that safeguards all data intended for global governance use through encryption and anonymization and processing through federated learning models. The local jurisdiction maintains control over its sensitive health and demographic information which enables global decision-making without any data transmission outside of its boundaries.

FACT: Research conducted by Brookings Institution (2023) demonstrated that applying equity-based dynamic distribution models would perform better than static GDP-weighted models by reducing COVID-19 deaths across the world by 30% while simultaneously cutting down economic losses in the minority countries by 50%.

Through PCED nations could join global surveillance operations for equity analytics without losing control of their data while being able to monitor its entire journey. The system will provide citizens with assurance that their data privacy remains protected from misuse or commerce while the population builds trust in the program.

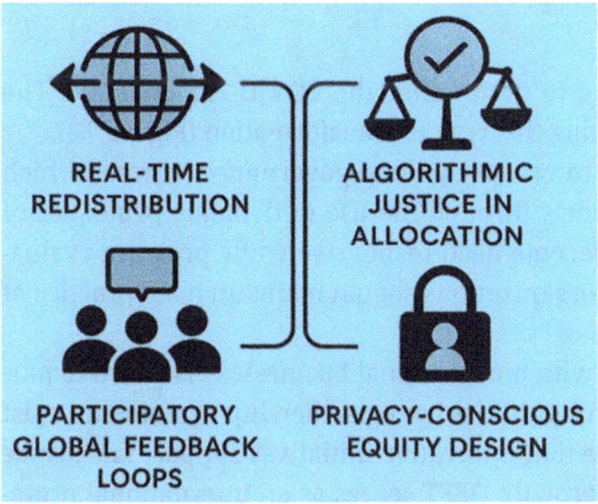

Figure 7.3: Pandemic equity framework.

Simulation Outcome: A Counterfactual Model

The Brookings Institution simulated in 2023 what worldwide pandemic operations would have appeared like through using an equity-weighted AI-driven distribution system based on its simulation model. A hypothetical analysis included DEFT concepts within a worldwide information dashboard representation.

The simulation showed striking results:

1. A global death reduction of 30% became possible through use of this distribution system.
2. The practice of vaccine expiration in regions with excessive supply could have been reduced by 60%.
3. The economic losses suffered by poor countries could have decreased to half their original value.
4. International institutions would have received an overall increase of 25% in global trust based on cross-border survey results.

DEFT's global utility becomes stronger due to these simulation outcomes that provide proof that demonstrates its practical value. The DEFT model demonstrates through functional outcomes that ethical equity serves both moral purposes and delivers operational advantages through need-oriented collaboration.

Lessons Learned and the Road Ahead

Future global challenges will continue to occur after the COVID-19 pandemic. The DEFT model serves as a guide for effecting this type of transformation (Figure 7.3).

International organizations need to create updated governance systems which build upon traditional compliance models through the use of dynamic principles of equity. The funding protocols should become need-responsive while program evaluations should include equity audits and organizations should maintain open practice of algorithmic governance.

Regional organizations partnering with multinational businesses also need to participate in these governance changes. All public-private partnership agreements must follow the DEFT standards to guarantee that innovative initiatives support fair justice outcomes while preventing inequality growth. DEFT serves as an international protocol which offers basic concepts and flexible implementation tools that organizations worldwide can utilize for cooperation.

Conclusion

From Crisis to Catalyst

The COVID-19 worldwide crisis exposed how unequal the existing worldwide governing structures have proven to be. This crisis demonstrates three essential lessons about unwillingness to act and systems that remain unchanged and nationalistic attitudes during times of universal risk. Such a global crisis revealed to the world a historic window of opportunity to explore fresh ways of handling shared problems as a single international community.

DEFT delivers solutions through its sub-theories comprised RRT, AGET, EFLT, and PCED as well as beyond simple critique. DEFT demonstrates how equity should be developed for the core structures and performance feedback loops that form the global governance mechanisms. The plan provides a pathway to establish justice systems that give premeditated justice rather than accidental outcomes or delayed responses.

The following chapter examines the process of institutionalizing DEFT across public and private domains to sustain ethical conduct along with participatory methods and data-driven approaches that will protect against forthcoming challenges.

The governments on the globe bring absolute change when they head towards the DEFT to fight the issues of global biasness and unfairness. They bring strategic development through their effective policies made with the help of DEFT. In this manner, the justice, accountability and fairness are ensured and taken into account in global communities. The DEFT systems make it essential to go for th4 equity unlike the outdated systems in the past. The collective use of the principles “AGET, EFLT, PCED, HVET, and TEST” makes the theory more effective in decision-making and policymaking globally. The global governance must ensure the proper use of the DEFT in their systems to combat the waves of the inequality and biased attitude towards developing economies of the world.

The DEFT also guides the different global and regional organizations to work for the equity. The different organizations working to bring governance change in the world are recommended to utilize this framework. The international and national corporations are also helped by the system to bring equity into action while ensuring fairness and transparency in the system. It further helps the government to identify the problems in the governance sector, offering valuable insights to resolve them. Moreover, it also estimated the future and make the governments alert about the happenings in the future. In this way, the governance can be improved by imparting the framework DEFT into the decision-making and policymaking at all levels.

Apart from it, the DEFT also offers wide range of principles to use and take the most of the technology. It suggests utilizing AI in essential decision-making procedures. The governing bodies must be equipped with necessary digital tools to further make the governance system more effective and reliable. The system of governments must be public friendly and ensure the fairness, transparency, accountability, equity, and ethical values.

Chapter 8
Implementation and Pilot Projects

Introduction

In this part of the book, we would showcase how the implications of the dynamic equity framework theory (DEFT) can be carried out in some of pilot projects which shows its practicability. These beginnings are in action to get DEFT from theoretical part to the actionable one. The DEFT is effective to use practically because the people who conduct research have used it in suburban areas to make reforms in the education, health, and environmental sectors. This shows its effectiveness and implications. Besides it, these assessment activities help the conductors of the framework to evaluate and implement the different but essential mini theories of the framework "AGET, EFLT and PCED", obtaining crucial response from the public as feedback to further ameliorating it. Furthermore, the chapter makes some updated and upgradations in the system that is functional across the globe. This further strengthens it in all its fabulous forms.

Pilot Program Examples

Education Reform: Equity-Centred School Funding and Curriculum Design

Location: Urban and rural school districts in South Africa and the United States

Context and Rationale

Education continues to be one of the most unequal sectors worldwide because it survived historical injustices together with contemporary socioeconomic imbalances. The previous system of racial segregation during apartheid in South Africa has permeated public school funding and educational access globally particularly affecting Black people and residents of rural areas. Public schools in the United States fund their operations through local property taxes which leads to major financing differences between wealthier and poorer areas where these districts usually operate in segregated racial lines. The DEFT framework specifies an objective method to address these inequalities through justice-based data analysis.

FACT: Per learner educational funding at South African poorest quintile schools exceeds wealthy areas funding by six times according to the South African Human Rights Commission (2021). The EdBuild (2019) reports predominantly Black U.S. school districts receive $23 billion less yearly funding relative to white districts despite maintaining equivalent student populations.

---

https://doi.org/10.1515/9783112222140-008

Pilot Overview

The DEFT education reform pilot programs utilize algorithmic governance equity theory (AGET) as a tool to distribute equity-weighted funding through its education reform initiatives.

Mechanisms of Implementation

Student-level data collection occurs continuously through analytical studies that combine racial statistics alongside gender and economic status and geographic information according to the DEFT process. The educational data enables machine learning models to locate priority schools that demand immediate attention through standards of insufficient facilities and high enrolments dropping out and substandard academic results.

To achieve optimal finance, the forecasting system for equitable measures utilizes the "weighted variables" which include the various sides of the classes and the availability of technological assets along with some proportion of academics in schools. All the algorithms used go through necessary audit procedures to avoid any bias towards results. This results in making things accessible and open to the public, ensuring fairness and transparency across all dimensions.

The parents of the students together with students themselves do interact with their mentors with the help of "EFLT (equity feedback loop theory)" of DEFT to make them familiar with the evaluation processes and their transparency. The feedback received helps in assigning budgets to the schools' expenses and the fairness in the subjects. The nature of amendments in schooling matters becomes obvious keeping in view the psychological healthcare elements.

One of the core tools used in reforms and transformation of academic activities, "TEST" plays a key role as it eliminated the inequalities in the academia that were prevailing in past. The ignorance of the innate cultural values and histories together with African inventions across the globe with the help of such academic policies makes the identity crises. The modus operandi offered by DEFT which unites the teachers, students, and historians as a team. In this regard, the group makes integration of academic and history to retain the real an original value of those culture that are the real part of the nations to acknowledge and value them. In this way, the innate language and other cultural components are restored with respect to different regions. The areas that had been on the verge of discrimination in past basically get recognized and valued with the help of "TEST".

Expected Impact

Through the educational pilots supported by DEFT the following outcomes should manifest:

The programs establish direct support for underprivileged educational institutions while adapting their teaching methods to match regional characteristics in order to enhance educational achievement of these student groups.

Students stay in school longer after connecting with the curriculum content and getting adequate funding that boosts their chance for post-secondary enrolment.

Healthcare: Dynamic Resource Allocation in Community Clinics

Location: Indigenous and low-income regions in Canada and Brazil

Overview

The public healthcare system in developed nations fails to eliminate healthcare disparities since its access benefits primarily non-Indigenous and middle-income individuals. The population of Canada and Brazil face unequal access to vital healthcare because both systems experience chronic neglect as well as historical discrimination along with clinic funding shortages. The existing social inequalities in healthcare services get worse because of cultural hassles that combine with distance from urban areas and limited health service planning tools.

FACT: News reveals that Canadian Indigenous people face three to five times more diabetes than other Canadians while Brazilian northern regions experience twice the premature death rates of their wealthier southern states.

The DEFT provides healthcare professionals with methods to develop localized adaptive healthcare solutions that put community leadership at the centre of service delivery. The pilot initiative uses DEFT to enhance community health clinics that will improve health achievements along with service delivery equality and public health system confidence.

Mechanisms of Implementation

The "holistic value equity theory (HVET)" of DEFT is utilized to get the thorough information because it makes the traveling distance aligned with the accessibility of the hospitals in the areas. It shows that it is necessary to have clean water of good quality along with good residential facilities comparing with equitable elements. The basic target is to disclose the ailing elements, highlighting the causes that gloss over the ways the diseases spread unequally.

The decisions related to the healthcare would be taken by the dwellers themselves with the help of "EFLT" that does it by spreading the surveys and interactions with the public along with some reporting stuff which is essential in collecting the feedback and ideas from the community. When patients join the loop they describe issues connected to travel restrictions and language barriers which leads to immediate healthcare administrator responses for solution creation.

The combination of federated data models and PCED (privacy-conscious equity design) puts patient information from such communities at risk of being misused through surveillance activities and exploited for political purposes. The implementation of DEFT enables healthcare data to remain exclusive within individual jurisdictions. The models assist clinics to conduct regional equity assessments without exposing patient information to disclosure. Organizations that implement encryption and authorization systems for anonymous data storage maintain full privacy protection throughout all levels.

Expected Impact

Expectations for this pilot project are high because DEFT's active guidance tools will result in quantifiable improvements in three key health areas: chronic disease care for diabetes and hypertension and maternal health prevention and vaccination services. The implementation of culturally sensitive and privacy-protecting systems will aid in developing trust between minority communities and healthcare organizations. The intervention's outcomes will advance current health equity standards while creating framework standards for additional community-based interventions in the future.

Environmental Justice: Participatory Climate Adaptation Planning

Location: Coastal areas in Bangladesh and low-lying US cities such as New Orleans

Overview

FACT: The annual climate displacement events in Bangladesh impact more than 4 million people (Internal Displacement Monitoring Centre, 2022) at the same time as New Orleans experienced 80% slower recovery rates in predominantly black neighborhoods when compared to white neighborhoods (Brookings Institution, 2018).

Climate change functions as a factor that worsens multiple challenges while systematically harming communities that have previously experienced discrimination. Coastal regions of Bangladesh and New Orleans experience aggravated flooding and sea-level increase and weather events elevated to critical levels because of well-established social inequalities regarding essential infrastructure and healthcare services and political engagement access. Adaptation methods that fail to address social vulnerability levels create empty environments which push people away from their homes and destroy their means to survive while enabling Swedish environmental inequalities to persist. Climate resilience planning receives its central focus within the DEFT which provides an innovative new method.

Mechanisms of Implementation

AGET Systems for Risk-Weighted Planning:

The AGET model from DEFT allows users to design equity-based climate risk maps. Programs merge predictions about floods and increasing sea levels with demographic elements that include population incomes alongside residential densities and population age ranges alongside evacuation resource availability. The system will direct Bangladesh's equitable distribution of embankment reinforcement funding and floating infrastructure installation while New Orleans can use it to decide the best position for stormwater systems and green infrastructure.

Using TEST (temporal equity shift theory) in planning allows planners to achieve reparative justice in their decisions.

The climate-vulnerable populations who exist today have suffered because of continuous pollution combined with displacement and disregard throughout decades. Planners can combine historical discrimination elements into their current decisions through the application of TEST. Areas in New Orleans which were displaced by Hurricane Katrina and industrial zones in Bangladesh which have faced decades of pollution would obtain support from funding assets according to their historical length of exposure.

EFLT and Inclusive Public Forums:

Decision-making processes in most climate adaptation programs consistently fail because they exclude those communities which bear the effects. DEFT establishes a requirement to place marginalized voices as the core decision-makers through participatory forums and community science initiatives and mobile engagement platforms. EFLT systems assess public input simultaneously to enable authorities to modify policy priorities according to the shifting regional priorities that range from storm drainage systems to emergency planning and post-catastrophe recovery plans.

Expected Impact

The implementation of DEFT as a pilot project for environmental justice seeks to lower climate-induced relocation while reducing severe weather health risks and strengthening sustainable community growth. Equity-based integration runs through all aspects of climate adaptation work including algorithm development and financial planning and community interaction protocols allowing communities to develop sustainable futures which uphold their history of mistreatment. The model contains fundamental elements which help various areas (Figure 8.1) establish climate justice systems at an international level.

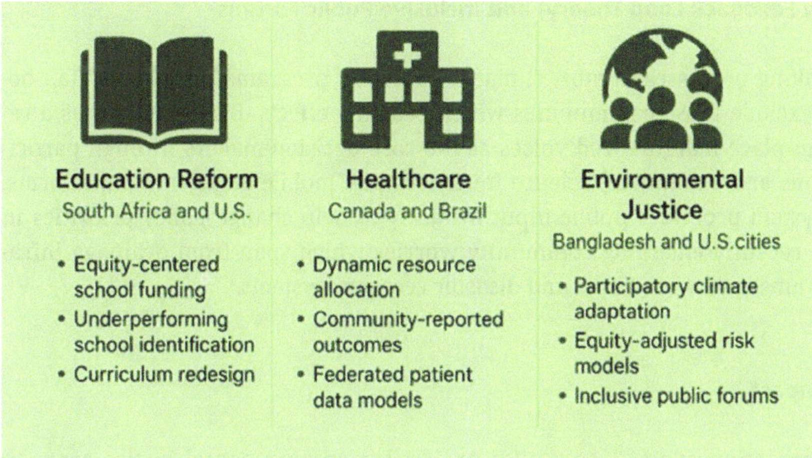

Figure 8.1: Samples of pilot program DEFT.

Scalability: From Local Pilots to Global Frameworks

DEFT generates power from established conceptual foundations and its most significant value stems from its ability to connect pilot-level community initiatives through various developmental phases into international administrative systems. DEFT requires a purpose-built framework with multiple dimensions because this will allow its transformative power to reach society at large, as illustrated in Figure 8.2. The implementation involves both territorial expansion and structural integration of DEFT principles into governmental decision-making bodies and technology development arenas as well as civil society networks.

Institutional Partnerships

The process of scaling DEFT requires the formation of strong alliances between governments and academic institutions with non-governmental organizations (NGOs). The critical supports needed for launching and increasing equity-based programs stem from these partners who operate both conceptually and practically. Government ministries should use DEFT concepts while reforming national policies through active partnerships with NGOs who act as community relation intermediaries to deliver feedback and academic institutions that analyse effectiveness and enhance strategies.

EFLT (Equity Feedback Loop Theory) and Inclusive Public Forums

Decision-making processes in most climate adaptation programs consistently fail because they exclude those communities which bear the effects. DEFT establishes a requirement to place marginalized voices as the core decision-makers through participatory forums and community science initiatives and mobile engagement platforms. The EFLT system processes public input instantly to help change policy priorities in response to recently emerging community worries which span from drainage infrastructure to emergency readiness and disaster recovery systems.

Expected Impact

The implementation of DEFT as a pilot project for environmental justice seeks to lower climate-induced relocation while reducing severe weather health risks and strengthening sustainable community growth. The groups make their future secure in terms of sustainability who previously have been the victims of the environmental degradation owing to inequity using this technique, since it processes financing and other essentials. The framework globally offers the methods that the countries around the world can utilize to ensure and enhance the environmental justice across the globe.

Scalability: From Local Pilots to Global Frameworks

The strength of DEFT emerges from its key concepts; however, its major plus point lies in the wellbeing of the community that it bolsters the projects that give boost to the enhancing the global governance frameworks. Moreover, it should be lifted up to make the revolutionary changes in the society that ensure the transparency, fairness, and equity (Figure 8.2). DEFT needs to expand beyond its geographic range while being implemented as a core feature of political decision-making processes and technological advances as well as civil society collaboration mechanisms.

Institutional Partnerships

The process of scaling DEFT requires the formation of strong alliances between governments and academic institutions with non-governmental organizations (NGOs). The critical supports needed for launching and increasing equity-based programs stem from these partners who operate both conceptually and practically. Government ministries should use DEFT concepts while reforming national policies through active

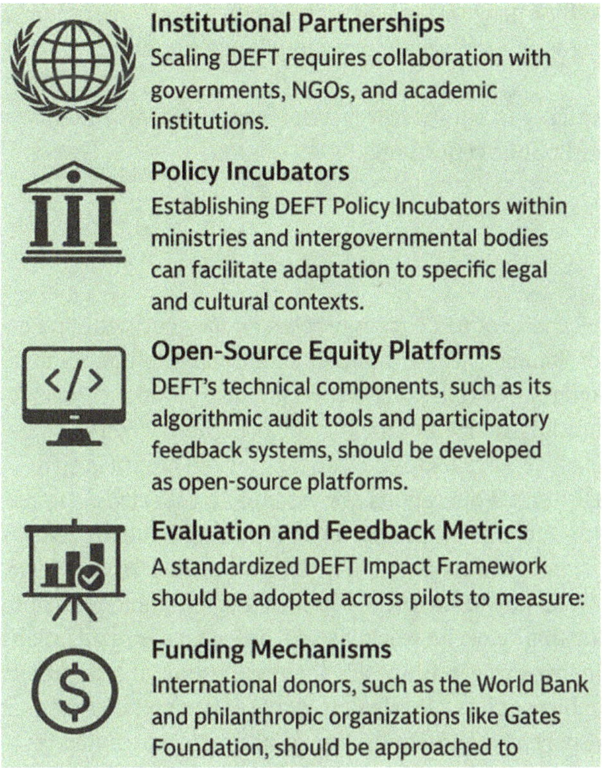

Figure 8.2: Local pilots to global: scalability.

partnerships with NGOs who act as community relation intermediaries to deliver feedback and academic institutions that analyse effectiveness and enhance strategies.

Authors developed an open-source DEFT Dashboard which combines real-time the equity indicators with public feedback loops and resource allocation maps for use by Jakarta officials and Bolivia health planners simultaneously.

Evaluation and Feedback Metrics

A standardized impact framework for DEFT implementations must be established because it ensures consistent accountability across various DEFT projects. The evaluation tools of this framework should consist of quantitative and qualitative measures which analyse:

1. The monitoring of time-related improvements in access together with results and representation levels serves to track progress for underprivileged populations.
2. Satisfaction levels of community members along with their sense of empowerment must be evaluated through surveys and forums and digital feedback platforms.

3. The organization should monitor program success through the implementation of DEFT's PCED principles along with local regulatory compliance standards.

Each metric needs to appear annually in equity scorecards for guiding adjustments to policy and academic research and public reporting.

Funding Mechanisms

The worldwide usability and applicability of DEFT entirely relies on the consistent and excessive funding for its further development. The concerned authorities like international organizations, "World Bank", should make collaborations with "United Nations Development Programme (UNDP)" for nonstop budgeting for the project. The partnerships between different parties must be made to have more sponsorships for the project growth.

The budgets for DEFT to carry on its operations are essentially collected from different donors around the world. The algorithms prefer community development as their first choice; hence they must be sponsored well to bring revolution into the world. The program works for overall wellbeing of the society in bringing equitable reform in many sectors. It is the core responsibility of the world as well as regional organizations to secure funds for this life-changing project. Proposals for the funding of this project are necessary and must be promoted across all relevant global forums; the combined effort to integrate fairness, transparency, and equity into healthcare, education, technology, and environment sectors is so essential that substantial financing is needed to ensure its long-term growth and development.

Conclusion

Developing "Pilot Programs" (Figure 8.3) is key to exercise the DEFT practically to taste the fruits of this amazing framework. The success of DEFT is clear when it is applied in the projects to bring educational equity by making complete educational reforms. Those in past have been involved in many discriminatory and biased decisions that were basically against the underprivileged groups' interests, favouring only few but the powerful ones. The implications of the system in different sectors such as education, healthcare, and environmental justice bring necessary equitable changes in these groups of sectors. In addition to it, it makes the revolutionary changes in the society that ensure the transparency, fairness, and equity in these mentioned sectors. DEFT needs to expand beyond its geographic range while being implemented as a core feature of political decision-making processes and technological advances as well as civil society collaboration mechanisms. The global governance can gain competitive edge over their counterparts in making the system fair and equitable, making the people treated equally and get recognized and acknowledged.

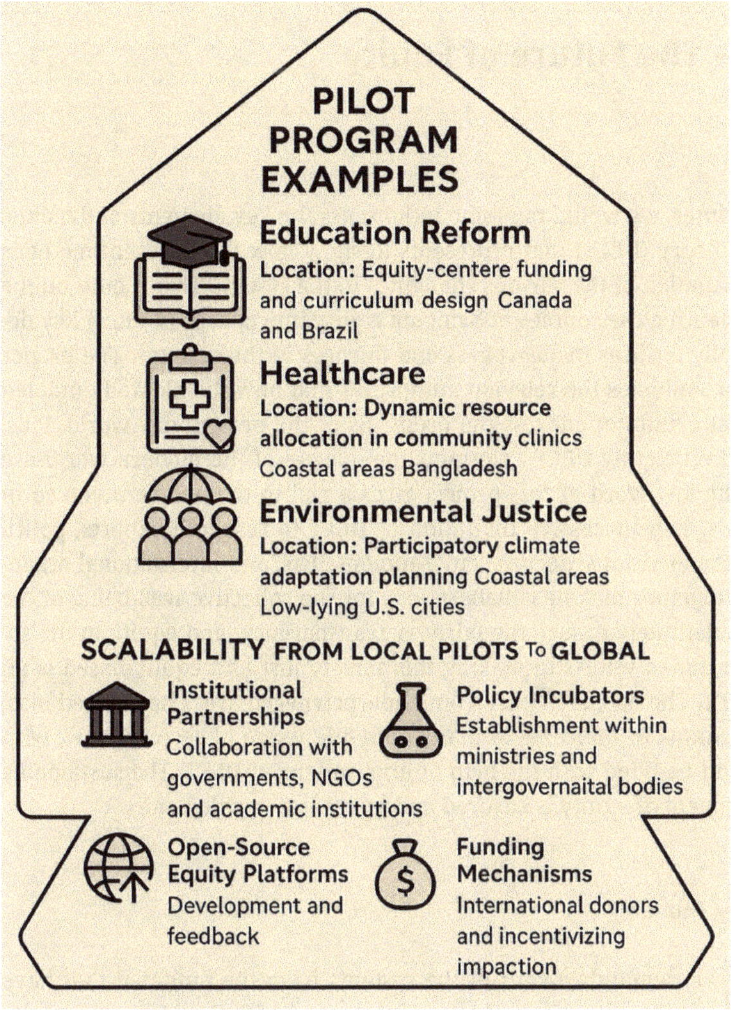

Figure 8.3: Pilot projects.

The implications of these programs help in building the strong public belief in the systems which is very essential for the governments across globe to win the confidence and trust of their people. Besides, it shows its effectiveness and implications of the framework. Besides it, these assessment activities help the conductors of the framework to evaluate and implement the different but essential mini theories of the framework "AGET, EFLT and PCED", obtaining important response from the public as feedback to make it further developed.

Chapter 9
Conclusion – The Future of Equity

Introduction

In the following chapter, we would pinpoint and discuss the key elements of dynamic equity framework theory (DEFT) that represents to show how the different methods are used in transformation of the various changings in the system. This is built on the principle of implementing the sources of bringing equity into charge in many key departments. It basically ensures inclusiveness and fairness in the systems. The proper analysis of DEFT recommends the relevant authorities that how the old and outdated systems used in past could not address the problems of the present-day world. Plus, how effectively and efficiently DEFT entertains the queries of the modern world are also highlighted. The last word of this project gives a call to the people involved in taking key decisions. The successive invitation of DEFT to research experts, politicians, economists, academicians, doctors, environmentalists, and international organizations to work in together making collaborations for the collective well-being of the society. This would definitely ensure the fairness, transparency, and equity in the social setting. The combined efforts to making this society just and equity-based is an ultimate goal of DEFT. The people in past from underprivileged areas have faced biasness and discriminations in the cases of many daily-life usage of sectors. Now, with this these gaps would be filled with the help of implications of DEFT. The sustainable growth and development of equity is ensured and hence it is in safe hands.

A New Era of Equity Thinking

The major framework demands a shift of the systems from the outdated that have been failed in addressing the current problems of the world with the equity-based systems that cater to the needs of the present-day world. The society this world is experiencing currently should be transformed from the previous systems to the new and real ones. The new approach is based on the customization. It renders the services according to the nature of the problems. However, previous system was lacking in this important factor. They were static, and only indulged in generalised and common solitons, while the modern problems need modern solutions that those have been failed to provide the needed resolutions. The society of this time requires some great approaches that are applicable and fit to each problem individually and address the hot issues of economic inequality, environmental degradation, biasness in key decision-making and policymaking, and digital accessibility. The fundaments of the equity are thus provided by DEFT.

https://doi.org/10.1515/9783112222140-009

The people who have been badly and differently treated in past in all walks of life in making decisions against them while favouring a few but powerful ones. When they are treated equally irrespective of their originality, gender, race, and colour, the equity is said to be practised, creating the way for brining equity and equal representation and rights of the underdeveloped people.

The framework provided by the DEFT offers key changings in the world order, as reflected in Figure 9.1, by prevailing equity-based systems. It blocks the inequitable behaviours from important sectors. It produces great results of the equity and ensures fairness, justice, unbiasedness, and transparency. DEFT considers equity as a functional; need and activity that fits to the current world issues and resolve them unlike the previous static models that could nit entertain the social issues people are facing today. Additionally, DEFT introduces a robust mechanism for managing equity across times and during revolution in the society, ensuring its consistent development.

The system for justice provided by DEFT actively responds to the social changes, making the financial development and environmental sustainability into action. As per the features of the principle, there is not any one solution to the problems. This model requires flexible systems to be carried out so that they may be fixed and fitted in different social settings with all necessary changes. These changes occurred due to population growths and geographic changes across the world. The flexible frameworks also needed for the governance systemic for decision-making and policymaking because the previously outdated systems have been in failed in providing needed results and are thus no more applicable in the current era of modernity.

To ensure the fairness, transparency, and equity in the social setting, the adaptable models should be used effectively and efficiently. The collective efforts in making the society equity-based is a target of the framework of DEFT. The people in past from underprivileged areas have faced prejudices and biasness in the cases of many daily-life usage of sectors. Now, with this these gaps would be filled with the help of implications of DEFT. Many theories of DEFT can be used to encounter the current changes in the world and face the problem of schools, hospitals, technology, and climate change.

The ethics should also be considered while implementing these systems. The people should not be discriminated on the basis of their origin, race, colour, or religion. These systems in past had been involved in making biased decisions, not favouring the uncovered and unreported areas and favouring those in power and charge that is temporary. DEFT however ensures that the systems do not make any discrimination using the assessment tools. These tools make evaluations with the time and if there is any discrepancy they find it out and try to fix them to provide fair, just, transparent, and equitable results.

The DEFT model allows the governments make people involved in the decision-making and resolve the issues together. When the governance bodies have to formulate any policy, they first need to get the policy-impacted people on the board. Consulting with them and getting their inputs into policymaking is the demand of DEFT to

Figure 9.1: The DEFT equity future.

ensure, ethical practices and equality. It uses "EFLT (equity feedback loop theory)" to get feedback from the people and make changes according to their suggestions.

The system for justice provided by DEFT actively responds to the social changes, making the financial development and environmental sustainability into action. According to "TEST", there is no any one solution to the problems. This model requires the governing bodies to use the flexible systems so that they may be fixed and fitted in different social settings with all necessary changes. These changes occurred due to population growths and geographic changes across the world. The flexible frameworks also need for the governance systemic for decision-making and policymaking because the previously outdated systems have been in failed in providing needed results and are thus no more applicable in the current era of modernity.

The DEFT model the governments engage people in the policymaking and resolve the issues together. When the governance bodies have to formulate any policy, they first need to get the policy-impacted people on the board. Consulting with them and getting their inputs in policymaking is one of the basic demands of DEFT to ensure ethical practices and equality. It uses "PCED (privacy-conscious equity design)" to ensure the privacy of the people involved. In this way, the chances of data theft are reduced, and the privacy is ensured.

This comprehensive book introduces the theoretical framework of DEFT followed by practical implications and applications. It adds essential real-world scenarios to make it more comprehensive and effective. The solutions delivered and shared by the framework are also included.

The new direction of equity thinking appears in the framework known as DEFT. The world maintains its constant state of motion according to this framework so equity must function as an adaptable process which alters as the world changes.

The twenty-first century demands DEFT as a guide to construct societies that evolve toward fairness and justice by meeting both human and planetary requirements. Society needs to accept dynamic equity because the present world demands fluid approaches.

FACT: The World Inequality Report (2022) explains the reason why adaptive equity models like DEFT are necessary since the bottom 50% of global population only received a 2% share of wealth expansion while the top 1% gained 38% from 1980 to 2020.

Recap: Why Dynamic Equity Matters

Today's equity-related crises surround us in the world because fundamental structural problems exist within our social governance systems. The problems which include income inequality and unequal healthcare access and environmental degradation emerged from systems created to maintain static order while being unresponsive to both fast changes and deep structural inequalities. Each static welfare model together with top-down governance and uniform distribution methods has an essential failure point because these systems do not understand why particular factors allow certain resources to be gained and who gets left behind.

Global problems today require new equity models because previous models have shown their shortcomings. The changes related to technological development in the world need flexible system to be able to respond them as there are various changes occurring in populations globally. Creating a system that responds to these changes is necessary because it adapts the changes occurring in the system in resolving the issues of the world. Their solution lies in the concept of DEFT framework.

The governments on the globe bring absolute change when they head towards the DEFT to fight the issues of global biasness and unfairness. They bring strategic development through their effective policies made with the help of DEFT. In this manner, the justice, accountability, and fairness are ensured and taken into account in global communities. The DEFT systems make it essential to go for the equity unlike the outdated systems in the past. The collective use of the principles "AGET, EFLT, PCED, HVET, and TEST" makes the theory more effective in decision-making and policymaking globally. The global governance must ensure the proper use of the DEFT in their systems to combat the waves of the inequality and biased attitude towards developing economies of the world.

The DEFT also guides the different global and regional organizations to work for the equity. The different organizations working to bring governance change in the world are recommended to utilize this framework. The international and national corporations are also helped by the system to bring equity into action while ensuring fairness and transparency in the system. It further helps the government to identify the problems in the governance sector, offering valuable insights to resolve them. Moreover, it also estimated the future and make the governments alert about the happenings in the future. In this way, the governance can be improved by imparting the framework DEFT into the decision-making and policymaking at all levels.

Getting DEFT into action in schools, the budgets can be optimized, and the funds can be effectively and efficiently allocated. This would enhance the financing of the education system that has been failed in past due to ineffectiveness of the then-used incapable systems. This method would use the ways to respond to the current issues and problems rather than the static models that were hardly resolving the issues at their time. This would moreover address the issues of imbalanced ratio of students to teachers that was created owing to growing population.

As part of its core purpose, DEFT helps in building equitable system of fighting the climate change. The biasness of serving only those areas which are not affected by the environmental changes would be eliminated. It would facilitate the affected areas for example in floods and allocate the financial resources to build resilient infrastructure.

The governance model suggested by DEFT is effective as it makes people friendly decisions and actively includes members of the public who were previously discriminated against in the policymaking efforts. It is an ideal to bring justice, fairness, equity, and transparent in the system. The contemporary governing system needs these reforms to make progress and development. The conventional system went flopped owing to using the outdated and practically failed frameworks that worked in the favour of only few, while hitting the majority hard.

The Long-Term Vision: A Global Equity Infrastructure

The "DEFT" responds actively to the ongoing insurgences in the world, making just, fair, and equitable environment across the globe. There should be an equity built that is perfect from ethical and moral perspective to the functional capabilities that combat the biasness and injustice and improve the living conditions equally for all the people.

The system that is operational at all levels of the governing bodies gets basic factors of equity for novel systemic approach to the governance. The social setting that is based on real equity that allocated their domestic funds very well and makes good commercial relations with the other world countries. At healthcare levels, the medical necessities along with medicines would be divided with continuous evaluations making it feasible and accessible for the weaker portions of the world. The adaptable framework uses the weaknesses to allocate the necessary and required resources irrespective of their geographic locations or political ties.

As discussed earlier, in the DEFT model, the governments engage people in policymaking and resolve the issues together. When the governing bodies have to formulate any policy, they first need to get the policy-impacted people on board as illustrated in Figure 9.2. Consulting with them and getting their inputs in policymaking is one of the basic demands of DEFT to ensure, ethical practices and equality. It uses "PCED" to ensure the privacy of the people involved. In this way, the chances of data theft are reduced, and the privacy is ensured.

The DEFT further requires normalizing the assessment procedures in many key decisions. In the case of budgets allocation, the systems must go through some necessary tools and evaluation stages to ensure transparency. This makes further system disclose the dealings to the public so that the trust among people can be built. The revised auditing process would follow financial auditing standards to create transparency and accountability thus making equity core to policy decisions instead of an additional consideration.

The extended time frame of DEFT seeks to construct an international equity platform which bases itself on raw data while engaging stakeholders through dignified practices that adapt accordingly. Through its structured approach DEFT establishes dynamic equity principles to build an operational system of equity for global society.

FACT: Adopting DEFT serves a crucial purpose because fewer than 20% of governments perform systematic equity assessments when making policies (OECD, 2023).

Many Sectors of Society Need to Collaborate Through a Call to Action

There is now greater visibility regarding the enormous task to build a fairer global society because many essential tools have emerged together with a shared determination to take action. We currently possess framework tools together with a general willingness from individuals to create a complex system of equity that serves modern interconnected society patterns. A sense of urgency drives this call for action which demands total involvement of every sector for its achievement.

Governments need to establish legal structures based on DEFT principles which must receive their immediate attention. Whenever any amendment is brought into action, the various sectors of the society should be bright into confidence before imposing any decision. All departments must sit together and make decisions that are collectively in their favour. They should support the common cause which is in their favour. Similarly, they should oppose the bill which is against their interests. In this way, the change can be brought by integrating and collaborating the various functions.

Figure 9.2: Conceptual Framework of Global Equity Infrastructure. A systems model depicting the four operational domains of global equity infrastructure. Arrows indicate bidirectional flows of influence between the central framework and its constituent elements, illustrating the recursive and adaptive nature of equity governance.

The United Nations along with other multilateral institutions and World Bank and international development agencies must transform their funding structures for aid and development and climate finance. International organizations can enhance their ability to resolve global inequalities effectively by moving past standardization of approach and implementing real-time measurement of equity. These organizations specifically help Global South regions whose systematic inequalities present the strongest challenges.

Corporations and technological firms need to actively establish their role in advancing principles from DEFT. These corporate entities should implement both the AGET and PCED protocols to transform their algorithms and data ethics protocols for better fairness. All modern computational systems controlling economic and social frameworks along with political influences need to have equity established as their fundamental design principle. Businesses need to establish equitable practices which combine complete visibility with inclusive policies that stop current prejudices from continuing or introducing fresh forms of discrimination. Companies can reach DEFT's core principles by conducting algorithmic audits and conducting long-term impact assessments and introducing accountability systems that support these principles.

FACT: The global average public support for government responsiveness reached only 43% during 2022 according to the Edelman Trust Barometer (2022) affirming that equity-based governance which actively involves the public should be vital for restoring social trust.

Our initiative welcomes partnership between civil society organizations with academia and philanthropic organizations for DEFT development through research projects and community-specific program implementation. Real-world implementation of DEFT depends on these stakeholders, see Figure 9.3 who will apply its theories to different cultural and geographical communities to achieve robust testing.

Figure 9.3: Global equity.

The non-compliance activities involve influencing the tax amount payable, including the act of declaring low income, undertaking activities and presenting fake claims of allowable deductions or filing of fake tax returns. Financial capacity that comes with employment standards and physical earnings greatly influences the ability of a person to avoid taxes. Hence, the financially weaker individuals are found to be more likely to indulge in tax evasion in cases of higher rates than those of higher-income levels accompanied by economic stability as they have more to lose in terms of legal consequences of their actions or the lack of them. Therefore, the effective use of DEFT can lower the fire burned.

Conclusion

Finally the Future Remains in Our Hands for Its Future Creation

The advancement of equity in upcoming days demands non-stop involvement because its productivity is higher and the humans are keen towards its output. The practical uses of equity require people to establish and utilize it effectively because it is not an automatic process; it requires conscious application. The actual equity is what it demands people who show sympathy and are flexible while facing numerous new dilemmas. It is an indication that provides the direction rather than offering static recipes.

The next path is to estimate the challenges and problem in the way of implementing it. The way forward to the dynamic and moving success is that we must put collective efforts and bring more participation and collaboration. All this must cover the finance, governance, society, technology, education, culture, and environment. It is not the end; it is just beginning of DEFT.

Actions speak louder than words. The real applications are carried out in the classrooms, hospitals, courts, and other public places. DEFT will come into action at these places because the public is there with governing bodies, decision-makers, policymakers, and scholars. This is the beauty of DEFT that executes as it combines all the people. The current mission of ours is to create a future of equity which is fair and just.

Chapter 10
Afterword: A New Path Forward

Introduction

The establishment of dynamic equity framework theory (DEFT) in creative ways poses problems for the static equity frameworks. It offers a flexible framework which bolsters in facing the current problems of the modern world and creating equitable environment around.

Inspiration: A Future of Evolving Equity

The aim was perfect of establishing DEFT as it was jointly met with will and strong mental abilities that helped in creating the system that supports and complements fairness and justice. It is the core need of the equitable set-up to get the world freedom from the old-used and out-dated systems that were governing the world for decades. Despite the fact that the previous theories had great start, they could not respond the queries of the modern world. DEFT proves to be the perfect replacement ensuring fairness and justice across systems.

According to this model the future of equity needs to be adjustable to match the changes that it addresses. DEFT defines equity through an active process which evolves steadily in response to fresh intelligence and evolving social trends and emerging community requirements. The future should establish equity as an active and perpetuating process which represents the multiple elements in diverse and changing human societies. The future will embed equity at its core DNA value for all organizational decisions together with their systemic operations and individual choices. The DEFT organization conceives of a society which positions equity principles as foundational decision-making elements responsible for steering all governmental policies from economy through education to healthcare. A future-based society will continue recalibrating fairness and inclusion as well as justice to provide each person with their rightful access to resources and opportunities alongside dignity no matter what occurs.

FACT: The upward trend of inequality has reached more than half of the world's population which totals 3.5 billion individuals according to UNDP Human Development Report 2023, therefore, demanding flexible frameworks such as DEFT which adjust to changing global environments.

DEFT demonstrates a pathway to create an adaptive flexible system of equity which grows alongside its environment and service domain. The vision presents itself as

https://doi.org/10.1515/9783112222140-010

both an achievable structure and operational model that can actively create concrete results. The basic principles of DEFT enable us to create governance mechanisms which adapt to changing circumstances by becoming flexible enough to improve continually. Systems adopting time-sensitive data and feedback systems together with decision algorithms according to DEFT continually adapt to societal and economic and environmental and technological shifting elements. The adaptation capability of DEFT helps communities prevent the drawbacks of stagnant ineffective responses while maintaining justice and equity for those who have faced discriminatory treatment in the past.

The implementation of a future where equity continues to advance proves difficult to achieve. The achievement of this purpose surpasses traditional theoretical methods or generic framework implementations. Associated with this vision are collective actions which require authorities to unite their efforts and share comparable commitments against established order systems. The DEFT approach does not provide instant solutions for eliminating equity-related issues nor function as the ultimate remedy for every situation. DEFT functions as a motivational appeal for every stakeholder group to unite for shaping a more impartial and equitable universal system. Developmental equity for total transformation involves partnership between governments and corporations together with civil society organizations and the academic sector and local communities who must drive the transformation towards equity.

All governing bodies need to place DEFT principles at centre stage by incorporating them into their official policy systems to help achieve the DEFT future (Figure 10.1). Government institutions should reevaluate their entire policy framework and evaluation measures to establish systems which guarantee their implemented regulations successfully achieve their stated objectives. Such systems need to remain dynamic so they respond to new challenges and opportunities because equity must remain the essential factor in decision-making processes.

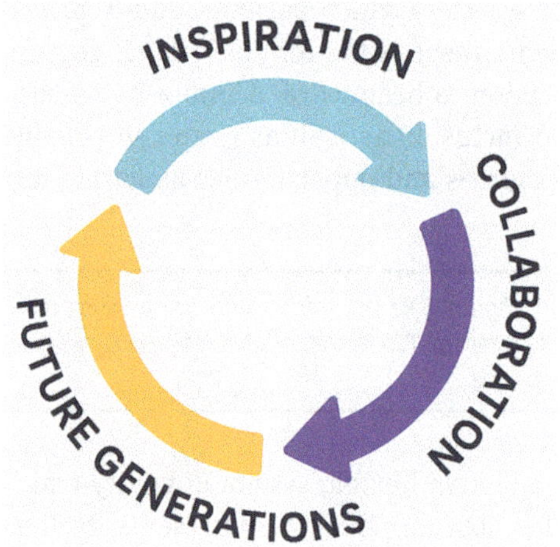

Figure 10.1: DEFT future.

The principles of DEFT need immediate implementation by corporate entities and technology companies that now control extensive portions of the world economy through their AI operations and data regulation practices. The strength of technology to increase social gaps matches its capability to benefit society in positive ways. Technology advancements will serve the public good when companies focus on equity throughout their design operations and implementation procedures.

Civil society and academic organizations and philanthropies must support DEFT through research about the framework and community-based testing of new approaches. Stakeholders need to monitor both national authorities and business entities to confirm proper DEFT principle adoption and continuous emphasis on equity across all domains of policymaking and implementation.

The process of transformation should prioritize the involvement of historically underprivileged local communities as its main focus. DEFT relies on dynamic community involvement since its members need the power to contribute towards developing the policies which impact their daily lives. Marginalized communities must have full participation in governance and design through which they add essential insights that enable policies to address their true needs and challenges.

With DEFT administrators change how they view equity by moving beyond static goals to create an active process of equity development. The approach demands changes to our policy design methods together with our approaches to resource distribution and success evaluation. It is essential to be dynamic and adaptable along with consistent efforts for learning more and more for to bring and ensure justice.

The implementation of systems which integrate equity principles from the foundation can deliver a future where societal needs remain aligned with fairness and justice throughout changes in the world. The promise of DEFT along with its potential stands to create an evolving equity system which we will construct with others to shape universal progress.

The Role of Collaboration and Shared Responsibility

The DEFT has shared responsibility as its fundamental principle. DEFT demonstrates that equilibrium in social equity exists beyond the capacity of either a single organization or institution to address independently. The achievement of sustainable equity demands multisectoral collaboration because governments lack the power to create it independently and businesses cannot resolve it through their social responsibility activities. True sustainable equity needs complete involvement from governments alongside corporations together with civil society institutions such as academia media philanthropic organizations and above all those whose lives suffer from equity deficiencies, as reflected in Figure 10.2.

FACT: Only 30% of low-income communities from across the world state that they have meaningful input in government policymaking processes (World Bank Participation Report, 2022) according to current statistics.

The responsible sharing of tasks forms an essential operational method within the DEFT system. Equity development requires people to share their understanding together with different populations and to make themselves jointly responsible. Legislators draft policies which require a complete alignment with actual social circumstances for their effectiveness. The role of advocacy groups consists of pressing for change; yet, they must achieve formal inclusion within the policy development structures. Corporate developments of technology and infrastructure pose risks to maintain ethical oversight and community consultation which can lead to increased social inequalities.

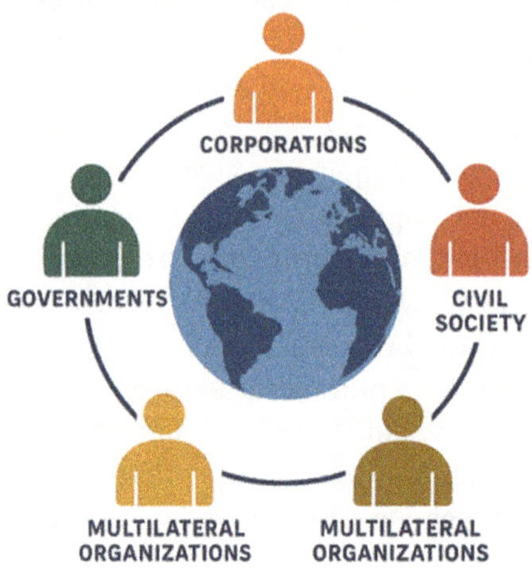

Figure 10.2: Global collaboration for equity.

Social factors also have key role in deciding to engage in justice-based equity. The educational levels, social trends, and personal interaction of the people affect compliance to justice. It is hypothesized that better education standards should lead to better compliance because the higher education levels indicate more knowledge of existing frameworks and the advantages of it. It is also true that cultural attributes and beliefs influence perceptions towards fairness and transparency. Another key aspect of this developing DEFT is to establish the kind of culture that is embraced by a given society, more specifically power distance, cohesiveness of society, and perception of authorities in relation to fair and transparent behaviours. The cultures that favour togetherness and obedience to the constituted authority exhibit low level of injustice. With special reference to enforcement strategies, it has been found that the legal mechanisms give direction to these attitudes. A competent system that is impartial and equity is essential in relation to improving the compliance. When individuals who consider system to be equitable as well as assume that the authorities applying the laws are non-bias and consistent, they obey willingly. Other components that are as well important in discouraging such discriminatory attitude include enforcement which can entail the use of penalties and chances of being caught. DEFT demonstrates that equilibrium in social equity exists beyond the capacity of either a single organization or institution to address independently. The achievement of sustainable equity demands multisectoral collaboration because governments lack the power to create it independently and businesses cannot resolve it through their social responsibility activities.

True sustainable equity needs complete involvement from governments alongside corporations together with civil society institutions such as academia media philanthropic organizations and above all those whose lives suffer from equity deficiencies. The development of active citizenship along with digital competencies and media literacy and accessible technology must be combined with interdependence practices. People who gain knowledge while developing power alongside creating organized structures are able to make institutions responsible and take part in policy-building processes that determine their life circumstances.

DEFT's dynamic equity model requires permanent societal cooperation at all organizational levels to be achieved. Shared responsibility requires daily practice to fulfil the promise of equity for the entire population. The long challenging path will become shorter through this design principle.

Transformative Potential for Future Generations

The DEFT shows immense transformative abilities towards future development. DEFT provides society with a fresh approach to achieve equity which transforms institution structures and economic frameworks and technological structures and community systems. DEFT establishes a framework which promises future generations to incorporate equity into their decision system and power-relations structures. Equity through DEFT functions as an ongoing development that needs sustained growth until it transforms into a society-wide administrative structure helping communities manage both complexity and unpredictability.

FACT: Equity-based proactive intervention techniques will become essential by 2050 because the World Bank Fragility Report (2023) anticipates that 68% of extreme poor populations will live in crisis regions.

Our present-day decisions through actions will structure the world which future generations will live in. Modern governance models and policy systems struggle to handle the stress caused by four major forces including global warming and artificial intelligence and changing populations and changing world politics. The implementation of adaptable frameworks along with foresight creates the conditions for reducing inequality that stems from privilege differences. DEFT was developed to avoid this path by creating tools combined with theories and mechanisms that engage real-time information together with community feedback while conducting ethical assessments. DEFT shows us how to advance our human communities through better determining the recipients of progress together with the decision-makers and voices of everyone involved.

Through DEFT future society will achieve sustainability combined with equity along with justice for people of all backgrounds. The future world will keep children from poor backgrounds from remaining confined by their starting point and enhance public health services to serve marginalized communities and employ algorithmic audits to stop discrimination in educational and work systems. Through its design DEFT enables public systems to evolve dynamically so they can adapt their policies before equity targets are missed which produces governance methods that function proactively and with sensitivity.

The vision requires both innovation along with imagination and courage to become a reality. We need to confront established unfair systems which claim to work in a neutral or fair way to select members by merit. Such leadership calls for moving from justice systems that handle transactions to systems that conduct structural changes. The method cannot deliver speedy solutions nor does it function as an absolute standard solution. This operational approach exists as a flexible system which communities of all kinds work together to refine through time. The framework has a dual transformative effect through established proposals and the inclusive process that lets all stakeholders join social design activities from basic foundations.

DEFT represents a capital allocation towards sustainable solutions for the future. The implementation of DEFT requires financial support for equity-focused pilot projects alongside feedback systems that include everyone and public education efforts and equity check-ups throughout urban development and digital systems. The development of new educational methods and leadership training programs should prepare youth to handle complicated situations while showing understanding towards others. Throughout history, future societies should not receive unchangeable systems that would fail to handle upcoming crises. Young people should have institutions that develop alongside them while learning from their experiences and operating under their oversight.

The envisioned changes by DEFT require more than just top-level directives. Communities together with social movements and regular people need to continue their long-term work of systematic accountability and better demands which generate grassroots-driven change. The duty to advance equity requires each succeeding group of people to lead by example while actively making change in educational institutions and government buildings and online environments and corporate workplaces. Equity needs to establish itself as both an ethical requirement plus fundamental design protocol and organizational habit that embraces social solidarity.

The selection of DEFT lets us create tomorrow instead of letting the future dictate our lives. The one of the best things of the framework is that it recognized and showcases the justice, transparency, and fairness before implementing, making it flexible and applicable to the modern problems of the world. As DEFT pledges to offer equitable, the upcoming people will surely taste the merits of the equity with strategic values and dynamics.

The DEFT will continue combating unfair, unjust, and corrupt systems for centuries for sure.

Conclusion: A New Path Forward

The development of DEFT is absolutely a landmark in the history of economics. It causes revolution as it converts equity into the most valuable and the much-needed activity for the world. Apart from it, this system is more effective as it fulfils the gaps created by the previous theories and systems for addressing inequality. By this, the community gain equal opportunities and learns to adapt to the changes, making its own way out there.

DEFT needs policymakers alongside institutions, civil society, technologists, and individuals to adopt this new framework of ethical decisions made with data-based principles which protect human dignity and involve affected communities. The principles of adaptability and participation and accountability from DEFT enable us to start dismantling outdated systems which we will replace with modern structures that represent true global community needs and diversity.

Employing this path requires extensive complexity considerations. The path to change will encounter barriers while the path forward is not expected to be consistent. Seeking collaborative approaches and accepting shared duty enables us to construct equity which guarantees permanent accomplishments in all our governance efforts as well as innovation and growth activities. The theoretical consistency of DEFT strengthens itself through its ability to invite collective action that supports tomorrow's co-creation as a group effort.

The journey advances from its starting point since this signals the moment when transformation becomes widespread. Equity takes root deeply into computer programs as well as constitutions, education settings, and residential areas. A movement builds fairness into its core practices to establish it as the standard for all operations.

The days ahead remain open and undetermined. The path ahead will depend on our commitment to perform actions and our capacity to envision broadly and include larger groups of people. We should advance this path with clear purpose and valiant spirit and equity forming the essential core of the story our forthcoming generations will create.

Appendices

Glossary of Key Terms

1. **DEFT (Dynamic Equity Framework Theory)**
DEFT serves as a flexible framework which inserts equity aspects into governance structures and policy frameworks and institutional systems to reflect evolving social development and technological systems and environmental conditions.

2. **AGET (Algorithmic Governance Equity Theory)**
Embedded within DEFT stands AGET which serves to build ethical decision-oriented and transparent and equity-focused principles in AI and algorithm-based public and private systems.

3. **EFLT (Equity Feedback Loop Theory)**
The governance system needs real-time community feedback about policies and programs to enhance their equity performance.

4. **TEST (Temporal Equity Shift Theory)**
This theoretical model integrates the historical discrimination with decades-long patient damages to present resource usage for policy production.

5. **HVET (Holistic Value Equity Theory)**
The proposed definition expands societal success by combining economic indicators with measures such as well-being and environmental health and cultural resilience.

6. **PCED (Privacy-Conscious Equity Design)**
The PCED principle provides guidelines for creating equitable interventions that support privacy and data sovereignty integration along with complete inclusivity and security and transparency features.

7. **Dynamic Equity**
The principle maintains that adaptive equitable systems should stay adaptive through changes in needs and risks since they require flexibility and responsiveness.

8. **Contextual Justice**
The principle states that equity needs to be identified and implemented through evaluation of community-specific historical background along with personal characteristics and lived experiences.

9. **Equity Infrastructure**
All systems to achieve equitable outcomes in the long term require institutions with technology, laws and citizen participation mechanisms and infrastructure for sustaining equitable results.

10. **Decentralized Equity Hubs (DEHs)**

https://doi.org/10.1515/9783112222140-011

Community-driven centres for data collection, policy feedback, and local governance that support dynamic equity in real-time and local contexts.

11. **Adaptive Governance**
A governance system must be adaptable enough to transform itself because of new data findings and public input and systemic changes that enforce equitable principles.

12. **Structural Responsiveness**
The capability of institutions to transform their rules along with strategies and resource distributions through different response levels for emerging disparities.

13. **Equity Audit**
A planned assessment technique evaluates policy distributions together with program or system distributional effects and equity goal alignment.

14. **Intersectional Equity**
This strategy assesses how different forms of identity-based inequalities such as race and gender and ability and class create simultaneous and intensified effects.

15. **Equity Calibration Protocol (ECP)**
DEFT uses an institutional performance indicator recalibration tool called Equity Calibration Protocol that changes equity-based measurements according to shifting needs.

16. **Inclusive Design Thinking**
Participatory design provides a framework which focuses on incorporating historic minority perspectives during service and system creation activities.

17. **Real-Time Equity Dashboards**
Technology platforms monitor and present equity data which covers healthcare together with education and housing and climate resilience domains.

18. **Equity Feedback Infrastructure (EFI)**
EFI represents the interconnected collection of electronic and physical processes for community engagement within continuous decision processes.

19. **Resilience Equity Planning (REP)**
Resilience strategies use REP to integrate equity into their systems while ensuring vulnerable people get first priority during climate events and disasters and recovery phases.

20. **Participatory Governance**
The political system which gives citizens particularly underserved communities the authority to oversee how decisions affect their lives.

21. **Legal Equity Mandates**
Public programs and funding must follow equity standards through mandatory legislation that defines evaluation protocols, implementation processes, and enforcement measures.

22. **Digital Justice Ecosystems**
The establishment of digital infrastructures with equity-focused components that maintains ethical conditions for online platform and AI system access and displays representative and fair behaviour.

23. **Transgenerational Equity**
The concept supports fair treatment of present and future populations mainly used for both environmental policies and fiscal sustainability measures.

24. **Civic Equity Networks**
Public equity outcomes are supported through collaborative efforts between grassroots groups and institutional bodies and advocacy groups that both encourage and track equity progress.

Article: Implementation Mechanisms

1. **National and Regional Equity Dashboards**
Every institution together with government bodies must develop interactive tracking systems that demonstrate sectoral equity indicators including education and healthcare and climate action and infrastructure services as well as digital governance systems. The dashboards should be available to the public through user-friendly components.

2. **Mandatory Annual Equity Audits**
Each year every public organization and their partner institutions must complete required audits for assessing their equity performance levels. The audit process evaluates both organizational data transparency practices and distributional fairness measures as well as access protocols and procedural justice protocols and corrective action systems.

3. **Creation of Policy Incubators for Equity-Focused Innovations**
The implementation of specialised units named Policy Incubators should develop innovative equity solutions by testing new algorithms or policy models and interactive community governance systems in controlled environments with substantial feedback possibilities.

4. **Integration with Digital and Algorithmic Governance**
Every digital platform and system using artificial intelligence should plan and implement DEFT principles from the beginning. All AGET guidelines must be fully applied from the initial design stage.

Article: Accountability Measures

1. **Appointment of Equity Officers in Public Agencies**
Every major government agency and public institution must select a certified Equity Officer who ensures DEFT compliance through training programs and works with external auditors.

2. **Public Disclosure of Audit Findings and Performance Reports**
Every annual equity audit together with its evaluations must become publicly available through multiple accessible formats. Organizations must prepare reports which present achievements alongside warnings about trouble areas and propose remedies that should be executed.

3. **Penalties for Equity Negligence or Algorithmic Bias**
Officials should establish strict legal and financial rules to penalize documented situations that demonstrate systemic equity violations with exclusions, discriminatory algorithms, and unhandled inequality facts. The penalties established for negligence will lead to financial penalties and funding reductions as well as possible legal punishments.

4. **Community Right to Appeal**
Through an official system residents can file complaints and appeals related to dynamic equity standards with either watchdog groups or community organizations or as individuals.

5. **Independent Oversight Committee**
The monitoring of national DRA compliance and assessment of structural equity health will be conducted by an independent multidisciplinary body that delivers yearly suggestions to legislative bodies.

Closing Provisions

This draft lays out a foundation as a living model that reviewers and refinements will adjust through time. The institutional equipment and legal frameworks which manage equity issues need to adapt when the conditions and possibilities in equity space change. Ongoing ethical and participatory adjustments leading toward a truly equitable future for all.

Supplementary Resources

1. **Recommended Reading:**
1. "The Future of Governance" (UNDP Report)
2. "Algorithms of Oppression" by Safiya Umoja Noble
3. "Design Justice" by Sasha Costanza-Chock

2. **Open-Source Tools:**
1. Equity Audit Toolkit (available online)
2. Community Engagement Platforms (e.g. Decidim and Loomio)

3. **Case Studies from the Book:**
1. DEFT in Climate Adaptation (Chapter 8)
2. DEFT in Global Governance (Chapter 7)
3. Pilot Programs and Lessons Learned (Chapter 8)

Index

https://doi.org/10.1515/9783112222140-012

www.ingramcontent.com/pod-product-compliance
Lightning Source LLC
Chambersburg PA
CBHW061217240926
51846CB00006B/1256
* 9 7 8 3 1 1 9 1 4 2 3 4 2 *